From the Irish praise for *Diary of a Teddy boy*:

'During the 1960s, Scala led the sort of high-flying life that most of us could only dream of, and now he has written it all down. *Diary of a Teddy Boy: A Memoir of the Long Sixties* is his personal, and highly entertaining, account of the decade that changed the world' *Sunday Tribune*

'An unashamed celebration of all that was excessive, socially undesirable and wildly exciting about the decade . . . A refreshing and timely antidote to the deluge of miserable childhood biographies that have dominated Irish literary fiction since Frank McCourt introduced us to Angela' *Sunday Business Post*

'Enter the world of the sensational swinging Sixties. The drugs, the desire, the decadence. Deadly. Think of the music, the mystery, the mayhem. Deadly. Think of Jagger, Lennon, *The Saint*, the Kray twins, *Easy Rider*, Jean-Luc Godard, Jimi Hendrix, Muhammad Ali, *Hair*, Salvador Dali, Mods and Rockers, Cat Stevens, Roman Polanski, Vespa scooters, Diana Dors, Radio Caroline, Richard Harris, Teddy boys, Marianne Faithfull, the Playboy Club, *Cleopatra* and Led Zeppelin . . . Stepping out of your life and into the pages of *Diary of a Teddy Boy* is like getting out of a grey Morris Minor and getting into the seat of a Ferrari' *Stage Left*

'A veritable *Who's Who* of the swinging Sixties scene (and underworld). Scala was more than a bit player. He had his finger on the pulse of London in its helter-skelter heyday' *Lenister Express*

Diary of a Teddy Boy

A Memoir of the Long Sixties

Mim Scala

review

'The "long Sixties", as it is best called, embraces a period from the chronological mid-Fifties to 1979, when on 3 May the party came so abruptly to its end' Jonathon Green, *All Dressed Up: The Sixties and the Counterculture* (1988)

First published in 2000
by Sitric Books Ltd

First published in Great Britain in 2001
by REVIEW

An imprint of Headline Book Publishing

10 9 8 7 6 5 4 3 2 1

ISBN 0 7472 7068 6

Typeset by Palimpsest Book Production Limited, Polmont, Stirlingshire
Printed and bound in Great Britain by Clays Ltd, St Ives plc.

Headline Book Publishing
A division of Hodder Headline
338 Euston Road
London NW1 3BH

www.reviewbooks.co.uk
www.hodderheadline.com

To Freddy and Janie

This book is also dedicated to the following songs, and to the many talented and inspired musicians who wrote, sang, played and recorded them. They put a special kind of joy into my life.

'Because You're Mine,' Mario Lanza. 'Jambalaya,' Jo Stafford. 'Don't Let the Stars Get in Your Eyes,' Perry Como. 'How Much Is that Doggie in the Window?' Pattie Page. 'Green Door,' 'High Noon,' 'I Believe,' 'There Must Be a Reason,' Frankie Lane. 'Oh Mine Papa,' Eddie Calvert. 'That's Amore,' Dean Martin. 'Such a Night,' Johnny Ray. 'Three Coins in a Fountain,' Frank Sinatra. 'Rock Around the Clock,' 'See You Later Alligator,' 'Shake Rattle and Roll,' Bill Haley and the Comets. 'Earth Angel,' Crew Cuts. 'Stranger in Paradise,' Tony Bennett. 'Hey There,' Sammy Davis Jnr. 'Ain't That a Shame,' Pat Boone. 'Sixteen Tons,' Tennessee Ernie Ford. 'Cumberland Gap,' 'Rock Island Line,' Lonnie Donegan. 'Only You,' 'Smoke Gets in Your Eyes,' 'The Great Pretender,' The Platters. 'Chain Gang,' 'Unchained Melody,' Jimmy Young. 'Blue Suede Shoes,' Carl Perkins. 'Be-Bop-A-Lula,' 'Blue Jean Bop,' Gene Vincent. 'Bad Penny Blues,' Humphrey Lyttelton. 'Why Do Fools Fall in Love?' Frankie Lyman. 'Giddy Up A Ding Dong,' Freddie Bell. 'All Shook Up,' 'Blue Moon,' 'Heartbreak Hotel,' 'Hound Dog,' 'I Don't Care if the Sun Don't Shine,' 'Return to Sender,' Elvis Presley. 'Ain't That a Shame?' 'Blueberry Hill,' 'I'm Walking,' Fats Domino. 'Baby Face,' 'Long Tall Sally,' 'She's Got It,' Little Richard. 'Don't You Rock Me Daddy-O,' The Vipers. 'Cry Me a River,' Julie London. 'Tenderly,' 'When I Fall in Love,' Nat King Cole. 'Freight Train,' Chase McDevitt & Nancy Whisky. 'Lucille,' Little Richard. 'Bye Bye Love,' 'Wake Up Little Suzie,' The Everly Brothers. 'Good Golly Miss Molly,' 'Great Balls of Fire,' 'Whole Lotta Shaking Going On,' Jerry Lee Lewis. 'That'll Be the Day,' Buddy Holly. 'Reet Petite,' Jackie Wilson. 'Chantilly Lace,' The Big Bopper. 'Stagger Lee,' Lloyd Price. 'Guitar Boogie Shuffle,' Bert Weedon. 'Endlessly,' Brook Benton. 'Lonely Boy,' Paul Anka. 'Only Sixteen,' Sam Cooke. 'Willie and the Hand Jive,' Cliff Richard. 'I'm Sorry,' Brenda Lee.

v

'Shaking All Over,' Johnny Kidd and the Pirates. 'Only the Lonely,' Roy Orbison. 'Georgia On My Mind,' 'Hit the Road Jack,' 'Your Cheating Heart,' Ray Charles. 'Stand By Me,' Ben E. King. 'Take Five,' Dave Brubeck. 'Moon River,' Andy Williams. 'Let's Twist Again,' Chubby Checker. 'Wimoweh,' Karl Denver. 'Jezebel,' Marty Wilde. 'My Funny Valentine,' Chet Baker. 'The Locomotion,' Little Eva. 'Desfinado,' Stan Getz and Charlie Byrd. 'Da Doo Ron Ron,' The Crystals. 'A Hard Day's Night,' 'Can't Buy Me Love,' 'Help,' 'Hey Jude,' 'Please Please Me,' 'Sergeant Pepper's Lonely Hearts Club Band,' 'Twist and Shout,' The Beatles. 'Twenty-Four Hours from Tulsa,' Gene Pitney. 'Anyone Who Had a Heart,' Cilla Black. 'Honky Tonk Woman,' 'I Can't Get No Satisfaction,' 'It's All Over Now,' 'Little Red Rooster,' 'Not Fade Away,' 'Sympathy for the Devil,' The Rolling Stones. 'Hi Heel Sneakers,' Tommy Tucker. 'Johnny B. Goode,' 'No Particular Place to Go,' Chuck Berry. 'My Guy,' Mary Wells. 'Shout,' Lulu. 'Tobacco Road,' The Nashville Teens. 'The Girl from Ipanema,' Stan Getz and Astrud Gilberto. 'House of the Rising Sun,' 'We've Got to Get Out of This Place,' The Animals. 'As Tears Go By,' Marianne Faithfull. 'Parchment Farm,' Mose Allison. 'Go Now,' The Moody Blues. 'Leader of the Pack,' The Shangri-Las. 'I'm Losing You,' Dusty Springfield. 'Baby Please Don't Go,' Them. 'You've Lost That Loving Feeling,' The Righteous Brothers. 'Don't Let Me Be Misunderstood,' Nina Simone. 'The Times They Are a Changin',' 'Subterranean Homesick Blues,' Bob Dylan. 'Help Me Rhonda,' The Beach Boys. 'My Generation,' The Who. 'Keep On Running,' Spencer Davis Group. 'My Girl,' Otis Redding. 'I Heard It through the Grapevine,' Marvin Gaye. 'It's a Man's World,' James Brown. 'How Sweet It Is to Be Loved by You,' Junior Walker and the All Stars. 'If I Were a Carpenter,' Tim Hardin. 'Hey Joe,' Jimi Hendrix. 'A Whiter Shade of Pale,' Procul Harum. 'Dedicated to the One I Love,' The Mamas and the Papas. 'Forty Thousand Headmen,' Traffic. 'Ode to Billy Joe,' Bobbie Gentry. 'There Is a Mountain,' Donovan. 'Grazing in the Grass,' Hugh Masakela. 'On the Road Again,' Canned Heat. 'Give Peace a Chance,' John Lennon and Yoko Ono. 'Lionel Hampton Live at Carnegie Hall.'

Everything played at the All-Nighter. All of Blind Sonny Terry and Brownie McGee, Alexis Korner, Graham Bond and Georgie Fame, John Coltrane, The Modern Jazz Quartet, Louis Prima, Keely Smith, Fairport Convention, Nick Drake, Billie Holiday, Elmore James, Leadbelly, Little Walter and the Dukes, Dizzy Gillespie, Bob Marley, Minnie Ripperton, Elton John, JJ Cale, Led Zeppelin, Carlos Santana, Pink Floyd, Eric Clapton, Quincy Jones, Jimmy Cliff, The Wailers, Sly and the Family Stone, Taj Mahal, Tina Turner, Richie Havens, the G'naoua.

illustrations

Section One

Section Two

Chapter One

The Scalas were just one of a large number of immigrant families in Britain, eking a living from fish-and-chip, ice-cream, and barber shops. The Italian community in Britain at this time lagged behind its American counterpart. London did not have organized Mafia gangs. There were, of course, important Italians who had the traditional role of godfather, but somehow the greed and violence of the Al Capone era had not penetrated the lives of English immigrants. Emilio and Nazarina, my grandparents, were hard-working and poor. Then, on 28 March 1931, Emilio went to watch a race at Aintree with the stub of a ticket in his pocket for the second Irish Hospitals Sweepstake. The white flag came down, the tapes went up, the 95th Grand National got under way. It took 9 minutes 32.8 seconds for the tough little steeplechase jockey Bob Lylle to coax the tired but game Grakle past the winning-post. The enormous crowd went wild. They knew they had a winner in their midst. The first prize was for £354,724 12s 4d, and Emilio Scala won it and became an instant celebrity – he was, after all, the luckiest man in the world.

Emilio and Nazarina had one daughter, Virginia, and three sons, Josepi, Geofredo and Mimi. As teenagers they all lived at Hamilton Lodge, Honour Oak Road, Forest Hill. Hamilton Lodge was a mansion built on top of the highest hill in south-east London, with panoramic views from its Adams drawing-room of the Crystal Palace and the city to the south.

Emilio half acquired the house with his new-found wealth, saying goodbye forever to the family's two rooms above the Battersea ice-cream shop.

As family folklore had it, Emilio had worked his way to England, leaving Isola del Liri, his home town in southern Italy, in the 1890s to follow the circus. This took him to Rome where, as a teenager, he busked a living with other urchins. He would walk up and down the Spanish Steps on his hands. This muscular youth caught the eye of a painter called Mantegna, after the fifteenth-century master. He took Emilio off the streets and employed him as a model. When Emilio had enough money saved, he made his way to London where he became an artist's model at the Slade. Then he sent for his childhood sweetheart, Nazarina Varaloni, and they started a small ice-cream business, selling their *gelato* from a tricycle in the then-fashionable Battersea Park. To this life my father, Geofredo Scala, was born.

As young men in the 1930s, Emilio's sons, Joe and Geofredo, cut quite a dash in the Italian community of London (Mimi had died young of bronchial pneumonia). My mother had fallen hook, line and sinker for Geofredo, with his dapper suits and good looks. They married in an extravagant ceremony in St George's Cathedral, Southwark. Granddad Emilio spared nothing, going so far as to import Swiss Guards from the Vatican for good luck. The wedding feast was documented in the English and Italian newspapers. The newlyweds moved in with the Scala family at Hamilton Lodge, which could easily contain all Emilio's offspring and their families.

I was born into this atmosphere on 13 July 1940. My earliest recollection of the house is of the enormous kitchen with its huge Victorian cast-iron range where all the Scala women and kids spent most of their lives. The kitchen was for cooking and ironing, and for pets and children. Chickens would wander in from the garden while fresh ricotta goats' cheese dripped from

2

small wicker baskets in the scullery and drying pasta hung from rods on the ceiling. The smell was a delicious combination of fresh coffee, baking bread and ragout. My dad was the young master of a classical Victorian billiard-room, where I used to love to hide under the table listening to the soft clink of the balls. Dad was good – a Borough-and-Watts finalist several times – at both billiards and snooker. The rest of the house was Granddad's domain.

In September 1939 Britain had gone to war. Granddad was interned on the Isle of Man with his friend Charlie Forte, because, as Italians, they were potential collaborators. He had sent Mussolini a telegram when he won the Irish Hospitals Sweepstake, telling him that there was an Italian in London who was also doing rather well. His sons, however, were drafted into the British army, leaving my grandmother, mother and Auntie Millie behind to run the ice-cream parlour on the North End Road which Emilio had bought for his children in the mid 1930s. Dad's education at Pitman's College stood him in good stead and he joined the Royal Engineers. Although he was not officer material, being just five foot two, he soon earned the distinction of becoming the shortest sergeant-major in England. My grandmother was in bits, with her two remaining sons fighting the war and her husband a prisoner of the country that they were fighting for. Then the bombs came. The parlour took a direct hit. Forest Hill and Peckham were pasted. Granny Scala, my mother and Auntie Millie whisked us all off to a house in Rotherglen on the outskirts of Glasgow, where we stayed until the end of the war.

By this time Mum wanted her independence and was fed up living with her in-laws. The three of us – Mum, my little brother Bernard and I – returned to London and a bombed-out business, where she chose to move from the luxury of Hamilton Lodge to a dinky little prefab in Hammersmith.

The prefabs were designed and built as temporary accommodation. Ours was one of eight on a plot of cleared land that sloped down to the river Thames. Only a few years earlier it had been a neat little row of two-up two-down houses, occupied by the workers at the Mambury and Garton sugar factory and distillery. A German doodlebug had flattened the block. The women workers clattered to their jobs at the factory in wooden clogs past eight little gardens with eight little rectangular, single-storey, two-bedroom dwellings made of sheet asbestos. They were hi-tech contraptions, with Bakelite and Formica fittings. Everything in the British prefab – ironing-boards and tables included – folded away. They were, however, warm and cosy. Each had a plot of land, an asbestos shed and a mound of topsoil to make into a garden . . .

Sitting on the precarious roof of the bombed-out factory at the end of Distillery Lane with my brother and a gaggle of other kids, we held our fingers in our ears as the entire remaining British air force, Spitfires, Lancasters and B-52s, flew low in victory over London, so low we felt that we could touch them. We waved, convinced that our dad was in one of the planes, and we were right. Dad returned in his grey demobilization suit with a kit-bag. He was back from Burma – with jaundice and malaria, but happy to be home. He recovered soon enough and set about rebuilding his bombed-out ice-cream parlour.

The war was over, people were cheerful, Dad was earning money. I knew this because a Ford motor-car appeared. It was square and black with a thin red line decorating the side of its shining bodywork, and it had seats of dark green leather that smelled of polish. My brother and I would sit in it for hours, parked in our postage stamp of a garden.

Our first outing in this marvellous machine came on my birthday in July 1946, my pockets jingling with sixpences and shillings – presents from various visitors. I climbed into the crowded back seat with my brother Bernard and my cousin

Laura and onto the laps of Laura's mum and dad, Freddie and Laura Varaloni. Mum sat proudly in the front seat as Dad drove the overfilled little Ford into the night. This is the first journey I remember making with my dad, bouncing about on Uncle Freddie's and Auntie Laura's laps, squealing with excitement as the little car drove sedately through Hammersmith Broadway and towards a different world, cruising at what we thought was great speed through Kensington High Street. Mum and Auntie Laura ooh'd and aah'd as we passed the big stores, C&A and Barkers, their windows dressed and illuminated for our benefit. As we passed the Royal Albert Hall and the Albert Memorial, I remember asking if the memorial was one of the Seven Wonders of the World.

The women wanted to drive by Harrods. Dad made the appropriate manoeuvres and we drove slowly past the greatest store in the world. The women talked about it in such reverent tones that for years I thought God must have lived there. More ecstatic mumblings came as we passed Harvey Nichols with its windows crammed full of bolts of material and overdressed tailors' dummies. We slowed down at Hyde Park Corner so that Dad could point out the bronze figure of a naked warrior. 'Your granddad modelled for that statue.'

We drove around Boadicea's Arch twice more so that we could see the effigy of our very own granddad, and then continued our journey along Piccadilly. The pavements were teeming with American soldiers, some in immaculate uniforms, others in their civvies. Mum and Auntie Laura seemed very interested in the clothes worn by the women talking to the soldiers. They all looked very pretty to me. Dad said that they were 'brass'. I didn't understand what he meant or why my uncle was laughing.

Suddenly through the misty windows I saw the most magical thing: a whole row of buildings covered in electric lights that moved round and round and up and down, flashing and sparkling, lighting up the street in greens, yellows and reds. In the middle of the street on a beautiful bronze pedestal was a naked boy standing on one leg, firing a bow and arrow. We pressed our noses to the windows to drink in Piccadilly Circus. 'Can we see the animals and the clowns?' my little brother asked.

We drove into Shaftesbury Avenue and turned off into Windmill Street. The pavement was packed with soldiers standing in groups, smoking cigarettes and talking to the pretty girls. Everybody seemed to be laughing. Dad parked the car in what I now know as Ham Yard and we all bundled out. I put my young feet on the cobbles and took my first step into the marvellous and mysterious world of Soho.

Our first stop was the Regent Ice-Cream Parlour. My parents, uncle and auntie were welcomed with open arms by the *padrone*, who was related to a distant cousin. His face was familiar to us from weddings and funerals. We kids were given window seats and were soon devouring ice-cream sundaes while the grown-ups talked and drank coffee.

Through the glass that reflected flashing neon lights I watched in wonder the throng of buskers, soldiers and girls on the pavement. My eyes nearly popped out of my head when I saw a black man in a duck-egg blue zoot suit, flashing white teeth from a huge mouth as he laughed. We were soon ushered back onto the street by Mum in her printed floral frock. She led us through the neon entrance of the Windmill Newsreel Theatre with its wall-to-wall posters of Mickey Mouse, Donald Duck, Bugs Bunny and pictures of a raft falling down a waterfall. In we went. Dad bought tickets, which a uniformed man tore in half, and we followed a beam of torchlight into plush red seats.

We had come in halfway through the film. I was spellbound. I slid into my seat clutching a bag of popcorn and watched in amazement as the voice of the narrator took me over the rapids of a river in the Yukon. I could feel the spray as the crazy craft reared and dipped in the wild, white water. When it was over, the lights in the theatre came on briefly, then dimmed again. Mickey Mouse, Donald Duck and Bugs Bunny all appeared on the screen, and then a Pathé Newsreel of the Derby at Epsom. The grand finale showed pictures of the Royal Air Force and all the British and American planes flying over London.

My head reeling from the magic of the cinema, I stepped back onto the streets of Soho. We walked through the crowds to Uncle Victor's amusement arcade in Old Compton Street. My grandmother's brother's arcade was shabby but exciting. It had bare floorboards, a row of pinball tables and lots of machines on the walls with spring-loaded silver hammers, which you flicked to send steel balls around a sort of maze. When they reached the top, the silver balls tumbled down through a battery of small nails, bouncing and tumbling until they finally disappeared through a hole with a number on it. If you were lucky a few pennies sometimes dropped into a tray. Uncle Victor, his hands green from handling thousands of copper pennies, gave us kids a stack each and let us loose on the machines. I spent my money trying to pick up a weighted-down, silver-looking wristwatch. The chromium-plated, cranelike contraption would never quite grip the watch, although for a moment I watched the steel claws close on the prize. I held my breath in anticipation. Of course the watch would slip back into its nest. All I ever won was the odd jellybean. I got to know that watch very well over the next few years. It was an Omega with see-in-the-dark numbers.

While the grown-ups sat in the back room where they drank coffee and laughed and talked, we kids ran between the legs of GIs and their girls. I was amazed at the way they could smoke cigarettes and chew gum at the same time. The GIs were very generous, and I finished up with a lump of gum the size of a golf ball in my mouth. My mother noticed and made me spit it out, saying that if I swallowed it, the gum would wind itself around my heart and I'd die. I stopped chewing gum for a while after that. Soon, three very sleepy children were dozing in the back of the car. I drew Mickey Mouse with my finger on the steamed-up back window, then fell asleep dreaming of Donald Duck. These monthly visits to Soho were to continue for several years.

Sometimes Dad would take my brother and me, leaving Mum at home. On these occasions he'd play cards with Uncle Victor, leaving us to explore. Bernie and I would sit on the steps of a place that had exciting music floating up from its basement, listening and wondering at what went on in the dark room at the bottom of the El Macambo staircase.

It was to be seven or eight years before I'd find out.

Chapter Two

My first school was a Marist Convent in the Fulham Road. My memories of this school are not good. Being a wilful youngster, I was whacked with a strap, a spoon, and by the tongue of the sadistic Sister Seraphina. The white angel wings she wore for a head-dress did a lot to disguise a basic child-abusing monster. Thankfully, I was taken out of there and at the age of eight I went to a delightful little school in Brook Green. Now that I could cycle home through the back streets of Hammersmith, my independence grew.

Distillery Lane backed onto the Thames between Hammersmith and Putney Bridge, and I was soon familiar with all the mysteries that a big river and its towpath could provide. Before I was ten I knew every nook and cranny of the river from Putney to Barnes. My brother and I, with a few of the more adventurous kids from the prefabs, would cross Hammersmith Bridge to the derelict estate of the late Lord Ranelagh. Its vast gardens ran from the Harrod's Depository by the bridge to the Star and Garter in Putney. Once over the wall, we were in wonderland. The ruins consisted of the huge main house, several cottages, and a stableyard with stone-built loose boxes. In the overgrown gardens were lakes and ponds full of large ornamental fish which we could catch at our leisure. There were territories in the grounds that we had gang wars over, and tree houses shared with kids from Barnes, Putney and Hammersmith. Usually we were chased off by the police or grown-ups until the next holiday or weekend when we would be back.

Our other secret place was more dangerous, inhabited by bigger, more aggressive boys who would hurt us if they were crossed. This was the Chinese garden that used to exist beside the White City Stadium. Derelict and overgrown, this oriental folly on several acres was a magical place to play in for any boy brave enough to venture over its barbed wire and jagged glass-topped wall.

Dad was rebuilding the shop, which had taken a hammering during the Blitz. Slowly it took shape until one day in 1952 he piled us all into the car to see our new home in the North End Road, and we moved into the flat above.

Dad and Uncle Joe ran the family business, Scala's Ice-Cream Parlour, 387 North End Road, Fulham. Granddad would show up once a week in his Lancia sedan, an astrakhan collar on his overcoat and a Homburg on his head. Although a millionaire by today's standards, once at the shop he would exchange these clothes for his white coat and white Wellington boots, and make the week's supply of ice-cream.

Scala's Ice-Cream Parlour was state-of-the-art, with pale blue, yellow and black Vitrolux mirror tiles. The lighting was of course neon, and three Deco ceiling chandeliers of multi-coloured neon strips illuminated the place and its terrazzo mosaic floor. The counter, in yellow and black glass, finished in stainless steel, was gorgeous. The soda fountain and coffee-machines were also chromium. At the front of the shop, facing the Market, was the ice-cream kiosk, a vast slab of stainless steel with six lids set into it. Underneath, the ice-cream was mixed and stored in five-gallon drums, which floated in a vast tank of freezing brine, ready to serve the endless queues that formed every day. Scala's ice-cream was the best in London.

I instantly fell in love with the Market. In the early Fifties the Market was worked by costermonger families who had been associated with it since the early eighteenth century (the Kings, Gads, Lees, Frosts and Hurrens). I loved its routine and its atmosphere. We were one large, organic, friendly family. The Market awoke early, particularly on a Saturday. The regular stall-holders would pull their stalls to their pitches while the lorries went to Covent Garden to score the day's fresh fruit and veg. The lorries returned at seven, and then the dressing of the stalls began. The carefully loaded fruit-and-veg stalls, the rows of polished apples, the stylized price-cards with their numerals drawn in chalk, were things of beauty. While this was happening the secondary traders would arrive to set up. By eight-thirty the first shoppers were on their way down the half-mile-long Market.

Dad's ice-cream parlour was bang in the middle, with the enticing smell of Gaggia coffee wafting over the pavement. More than fifty thousand shoppers must have hustled and bustled their way past our door by the end of the day. In summer most of them would queue for ice-cream.

By six o'clock it was all over. Great piles of market detritus littered the empty street. The bigger the piles, the more successful the day had been. Late evening was for the scavengers to pick their way through the leftovers. Clever women would leave with a pramful of slightly soiled fruit and veg. Next came the cleaners, a cheerful bunch and very much part of the Market family. By eight o'clock the road was as clean as a country high street. The Market pubs were full, the pianos rocking, and the mild and bitters cascading like Niagara Falls.

I remember my fourteenth birthday. It was a Saturday in 1954, in the middle of a July heat wave. The ice-cream queue had formed at half past seven in the morning and was still snaking down Anselm Road at lunchtime. I kept hoping that my dad would suddenly say 'Happy Birthday' and give me my present.

11

We were so busy no one took a lunch break with four of us – Uncle Gerald, Uncle Freddie, Auntie Tina and myself – whacking out handmade wafers and cornets.

In the late afternoon Dad sent me on an errand to Lillie Road to collect his billiard cue, which was being re-tipped. I strolled through the Market on my errand and went to the address I had been given, walking into the workshop of master craftsman and racing-bike builder, Mr H.E. Green. He and Mr Charles Holdsworth of Putney built the best bespoke racing bikes in London. These bikes had made-to-measure frames and imported Italian aluminium fittings, with beautiful gothic curls on the frame lugs and lightweight wheels. They were works of art.

'Let's have you then, son,' said Mr Green. 'Sit on this one, and I'll measure you up.'

My hand-built H.E. Green racing bike took a month to make. When it was delivered, I felt like the king of the world. Soon I was kitted up and racing. By now I had graduated to St Edmund's secondary school in St Dunstan's Road, Hammersmith. Naturally I rode my best bike to school until, just before the Christmas holidays, it was stolen.

The loss of that bike changed my world. I started spending more time on street corners. Stand on one long enough and you will see and understand all the mysteries of life. A good street corner has no prejudice. We learned about sex, crime, society, sport. In Fulham the street corner, not school or our mum's kitchen, became the centre of our universe. This was where we learned everything. The street corner was our Internet.

I hung around with the big boys and their girls. I fell in heart-thumping love with every beautiful girl who talked to me. A good crush could last for weeks and would dominate all actions. At the end of the day you either had It or you didn't and I wanted whatever It was.

It was 1956 and I was almost sixteen. I could not read,

write or spell. I was hopeless at football, fair at cricket, a fanatical fisherman and a racing cyclist. My only academic achievement was that I won the school prize for art. A painting I had made of the Crucifixion was hanging in the palace of a Cardinal Minsenti. Three of my paintings and a plaster-of-Paris mosaic had been accepted for the Royal Academy's Children's Art Exhibition. My best friend Howard Bond won the gold medal at the exhibition; I got the bronze, and two highly commended certificates dished out by Sir Hugh Casson. This was heady stuff for two cockney boys from Fulham. We had to go to Piccadilly to receive our prizes.

After the presentation we were taken for a walk through Soho to St Martin's College of Art in Tottenham Court Road. As a special treat we were given a guided tour of this real art school by a beautiful senior student, with long raven hair and paint-covered jeans. As she showed us around the various departments, and we rubbed shoulders with these budding bohemians, Howard and I suddenly became deeply ashamed of our school blazers. Tight trousers, baggy sweaters and sandals seemed to be the standard uniform at St Martin's. Once we were shown the street we found ourselves following a bunch of students along Tottenham Court Road until they disappeared into a place with a sign proclaiming itself The Gyre and Gimble Coffee House. We followed them inside. This was it. This was where the real world began: candles in wine bottles, dark corners with earnest young men spouting poetry, a beautiful, barefoot girl singing folk songs. We both became instant bohemians by turning our school blazers inside-out to reveal the striped lining. Thus attired, we sat self-consciously in a corner nursing a single cup of cappuccino.

To our amazement, Tina, our student guide, came in and went from table to table with a folder full of drawings for sale. Howard drew a brilliant portrait of her on the menu. Suddenly she came over to our table, said hello and sat down. We could not believe our luck. Tina loved Howard's portrait and swapped one of her drawings for it. I attempted one of her on the table cloth with a biro. It didn't impress her, but it did impress the manager of the Gyre and Gimble, who promptly threw us out. Incredibly, Tina came with us, and we spent the next couple of hours wandering around Soho visiting numerous coffee bars, by which time I had conceded that Tina was hopelessly in love with Howard.

He had the same impression, until, on a corner of Old Compton Street, outside the 2i's, Tina announced that she had to go and jumped onto the pillion of a Vespa motor-scooter driven by a big handsome beatnik with a beret. She disappeared into the traffic, leaving two love-struck schoolboys on the pavement with far more than their school blazers turned inside-out. Reversing our jackets, we caught the number 14 bus home to Fulham, and reality.

Chapter Three

Two weeks later Howard won a scholarship to the Slade; I did not. I went to work full-time for my father. Scala's had become the most famous ice-cream in west London, and my dad's parlour was the next best thing to an American drugstore. All American films seemed to have soda fountains with stainless-steel counters, mirrored walls, jukeboxes and, above all, wise-cracking guys in smart white coats serving up sundaes and sodas in long thin glasses to hordes of pretty bobby-soxers. I could be just like those soda jerks, right here in the North End Road. I began to grow my schoolboy haircut into a fully fledged 'Tony Curtis', which was only slightly bastardized by the addition of a mild Duck's Arse at the back.

To go with this new image, I commissioned Mr Tobias of 200 North End Road, a tailor respected by the discerning Fulham Teddy boys, to make me my first suit.

The dimensions of a novice Teddy boy's suit were usually governed by the novice Teddy boy's parents. If his parents were lenient and shameless, Tobias would have a free hand to build one of his more spectacular efforts. Shoulder pads, constructed to project eighteen inches outwards from each side of the neck, would be covered by a suitable material, black for the hard boys, duck-egg blue if you were into Johnny Ray, or a wonderful shiny silver herring-bone cloth, as favoured by the Walham Green gang. The collar of the coat was critical: a narrow strip of velvet had to curve gently just below the DA hairline. The ideal suit tapered from the extended shoulders to the trouser turn-ups, an inch and a half in depth and seven inches wide. The jacket was then cut to the fingertips ('the fingertip drape'); if your parents allowed it, it had flapped pockets, one breast, one ticket, and two for the hands to go into when lounging around the British Home Stores. In Fulham the buttons on a Ted suit were special: seven of them ran from the tiny lapel down the front of the jacket, the last one level with the cuff.

Tobias excelled himself: my first silver herring-bone was brilliant. I picked it up on my tea-break on a Saturday afternoon. It was a hot July day. The queue for ice-cream stretched down the Market for fifty yards. I worked away for the rest of the afternoon and into the early evening as the Market closed down, the cleaners moved in and the persistent queue slowly vanished. All I could think of was my first night out as an official Teddy boy with the Walham Green gang. I was going to be late for my initiation.

As soon as the 'CLOSED' sign was hung on the door, the family began the counting of the cash. I bribed my brother to help Dad, Uncle Joe and Cousin Julio count the money, which on a summer Saturday would fill a dozen or so foot-square biscuit tins with halfpennies, pennies, threepenny bits, sixpences, shillings, two-bobs and half-crowns.

I ran upstairs. I had no time for a bath, so, still smelling of vanilla essence, I changed into a white shirt with a flyaway collar, and a bootlace tie with a cow-skull toggle. Its red glass eyes were shining at me as I undid the box and took out my silver suit. I adjusted the braces of my trousers and put on the yellow socks. Then from under the bed I took out the Dolcis box that contained my blinding new pair of Jeff Chandlers: inch-thick crepe, crinkly soles, topped with black suede and finely decorated with thin strips of black patent leather, cleverly woven into patterns around the seams. Finally I climbed into the jacket, twisting my skinny frame to adjust the gigantic Mr Tobias shoulders. After posing for a while in the bathroom mirror, and adding a final squirt of Brylcreem, a liberal splash of Old Spice and one final comb of the hair, I stood transformed. The DA was flying, the suit was magnificent.

My one problem was how to get out of the flat. Over the past few weeks Teddy boys had stabbed several people to death on Clapham Common and staged numerous gang fights all over London. They were about as popular with parents as headlice. The only exit was through the shop, where my dad, my brother, Uncle Joe and Cousin Julio sat counting money at one of the tables. I could hear the clink as I stood on the iron fire escape that ran down the back of the building. I opened the door and walked with the swagger of a fully fledged Ted towards the exit. My crepes crept across the terrazzo floor of the café. My reflection in the pink mirrors enhanced by the neon ceiling lighting was a vision I'd dreamed about. I looked the business. As I drew level with the concentrating money-counters, one of them looked up. It was my dad.

'Where the fuck do you think you're going looking like that? Get upstairs and take it all off now.'

I made an instant decision. The traction of crepe soles on terrazzo flooring was brilliant. I began my sprint to the door. Dad jumped up, giving the counting table a hefty thump with his knee. As I fled through the door of the shop, all I could hear was the tinkling cascade of hard-earned coins bouncing and rolling behind me. A Teddy boy running is a strange sight. The shoes weighed a pound apiece; the thick soles slapped the pavement, compressed, expanded and propelled me forward as if I were running on a trampoline. I did not stop to look back. I did, however, catch my reflection in numerous shop windows. (Teddy boys were really narcissistic. I mean Masai-warrior, Beau-Brummell, Bertie-Wooster narcissistic.) Slowing down as I reached the Fulham Baths, I ducked into the doorway of

Radio Rentals to rearrange the outfit. Mr Tobias's shoulder pads were not designed for sprinting. I combed the Tony Curtis, taking special care with the DA, and made my way to the corner of Munster Road and the Star Café. This place was the original greasy spoon, so crummy that the Greek owner actually welcomed the Teds – something that my dad did not do at Scala's.

I sauntered in and ordered a cup of tea and a cheese roll. The chieftain of the Fulham Teds went by the name of Korky, as he bore a striking resemblance to the cat of that name in the *Dandy* comic. Korky was six feet tall, as thin as a pin and decked out in a magnificent black Toby. His very prominent Adam's apple bobbed above a plastic silver skull toggle, from which dangled a black ribbon tie. He was probably twenty to my sixteen. Next to Korky lounged Dumb-Dumb, a ginger mute reputed to be the hardest Ted in Fulham. I wandered over to the shelf that they were leaning on, put down my tea and roll, and checked myself in the Bovril mirror.

'Nice whistle, Scala. It's a Toby innit?'

'Yes,' I replied proudly, sliding my hands into the jacket pockets.

Dumb-Dumb sucked in a lot of air and made a string of sounds deep down in the back of his throat. He then produced a cut-throat razor from his inside pocket and neatly cut the bottom button off my jacket.

'He finks yer coat's got too many buttons,' Korky said, sipping his tea.

'Yeah, I fought so too,' said I, hoping that this was as violent as my initiation would get.

I waited in silence for the next move, nonchalantly sipping my tea. The silence was shattered by the spring bell on the café door. Scatter, Duck Lips, and Alfie Bates swaggered in. Alfie was a friend who worked on a stall in the Market, a few yards from my ice-cream counter.

'Tasty whistle, Mim,' said Alfie. 'Coming down the Brick-layers? There are some bints in there from Putney.'

At the mention of bints everyone started combing their hair. Korky commandeered the Bovril mirror, combed his hair straight back on his head and then pushed it forward with the palm of his hand until a suitable quiff appeared over his forehead. Slicking back the sides, he ran his finger down the DA for definition, and we were on the street.

Although there were only six of us at this stage, it felt as if I was moving with an army. It was amazing the way pedestrians crossed the road or moved out of the way. We swaggered into the Bricklayers' Arms, had a whip-round and ordered lager and limes. The girls were in a large booth, their bouffant hair sprayed solid with lacquer, lipstick trowelled on, eyelashes stuck on. In the snug booth they nonchalantly drank Snowballs as they cackled in pencil skirts with wide elastic belts pinching in their waists, and pretended not to notice the Walham Green gang. Snowballs were sent over the bar and were accepted by the bints with a sort of indefinite smile. The Teds, however, made no acknowledgment of the fact that they had bought the girls drinks.

The gang, glowing from the lager and limes and undercover flirtations, hit the street, pushed to the front of the queue at the Red Hall Cinema and bought tickets. A discreet look over one shoulder pad revealed that the bints were following; a look over the other shoulder pad revealed that outside the Fulham Baths was a collection of Teds from across the river. The Putney gang had followed their bints to Fulham.

Soon we were inside the cosy cinema, chanting for the fire-screen to go up, and ignoring the fact that the Putney bints had clambered into the row directly behind us.

The gang whistled and stomped until the manager wisely pulled back the curtains, wound up the asbestos fire-screen and brought down the house lights. The gang hissed through an advertisement from a bookmaker: 'You win when you lose with Margolis and Ridley.' Next came the framed cartouch for *Blackboard Jungle*, which had been passed by the British film censor.

What happened next changed my life. The overpowering and unforgettable sound of rock and roll hit me between the ears. After twelve bars the words 'One, two, three o'clock, four o'clock rock' came belting into the cinema. *Blackboard Jungle* had begun and Bill Haley and his Comets had indelibly stamped my soul. The incredible thing was that anyone who heard the song once immediately knew the first forty-three words. I don't know any other song lyric that contagious. I sat there in the Red Hall stunned at the behaviour of the *Blackboard Jungle* delinquents, my suede shoes tapping to the compulsive soundtrack.

Out of the darkness the silhouette of a Teddy boy flashed down the aisle, immediately followed by several others. Alfie Bates, sitting in the aisle seat next to me, screamed 'Bastard!' and jumped from his seat. Korky leapt across two rows of seats in pursuit. He ran down the aisle, jumped onto the stage and wrestled with a Ted who had run along in front of the screen with a razor. The bottom of the screen sagged open like a giant mouth. The cinema erupted into chaos as seats were ripped out and slashed: it was the Putney Teds versus the Walham Green gang. The film kept on running, the slashed screen giving it a surreal quality. The projectionist was in the pub next door — he always went for a pint between reels, as he told me when he next bought an ice-cream. The manager turned on the lights and called the police. Now at least we could see whom we were fighting. The bints were screaming and the regular punters had run for cover.

Soon I was out the exit with Alfie and running. At the corner of Farm Lane Alfie fell down and I helped him up. Blood was pumping in thin squirts from the vicinity of his ear. We ran down Farm Lane to his mum's house, leaving the chaos behind us. We finally stopped running at his front door. Back on the North End Road we could hear the sounds of the brawl, the echo of windows smashing and the bells of police cars and ambulances. Mrs Bates opened the door and promptly fainted. Alfie's elder brother Charley pulled us both into the scullery.

I stood there, my heart beating like a drum. The silver suit was ripped and hung open like a battle standard, covered in blood. None of it was mine, miraculously. Alfie had a razor slash across his right ear and cheek; it must have missed his jugular by a zit. His mum pulled herself together and sent one of her daughters around to get my dad. The next thing I knew, my mum and dad were in the scullery. Mum was in a state of panic, biting her knuckles with worry. 'Are you all right, son?' asked my dad.

'I'm okay,' I said.

Bang. He clouted me round the ear so hard that I flew off the chair and onto the floor, my head ringing like Big Ben, with my mother leaning over me saying, 'Your father is really upset.' Doctor Hubbard came around and sewed up Alfie's face, and then I was taken home.

Chapter Four

Disenchanted with the violence of the Walham Green gang, I soon found a new bunch of heroes to associate with, the bohemian art students on the King's Road in Chelsea. Some frequented a coffee shop in Earl's Court. The Troubadour was a magical place, the ceiling hung with all sorts of paraphernalia and musical instruments. After I delivered some ice-cream to the owner one day he asked me to give him a hand helping to arrange a stage in the basement. I plugged a microphone into a Fender amp and helped with the trestle seating.

The coffee house began to fill up. Sonny Terry and Brownie McGee, two conservatively dressed black men, arrived and walked directly onto the stage. This was my first blues attack: I could not believe what I was hearing. The harmonica wailed and screamed with a gut-wrenching tone. It had the same effect on me as Bill Haley had had a few weeks before. I would now always be hooked on the blues.

My life was becoming schizophrenic. I was still working for Dad but I had a social life in the King's Road. As a student I was eligible to go to the Chelsea Arts Ball, held annually in the Albert Hall, the last decadent fancy-dress party of the Fifties. Toffs had private boxes filled with champagne and food, while below in the auditorium the students went wild on Merrydown cider.

One of the models in the life class was a buxom girl called Lulu. She took a shine to me and one day asked me to come to

Soho with her. She took me to Jimmy the Greek's, a basement at the foot of Greek Street. Here she fed me estifado, olives, chillies, baklava, and two bottles of Greek wine. I had never felt so good, or so in love.

Lulu dropped me off at the 2i's coffee bar in Old Compton Street saying that she had a bit of business to attend to. The 2i's was famous as the heart of English rock and roll. Tommy Steele, Billy Fury and Terry Dene all performed there. Between sets they worked behind the counter dispensing orange juice and cappuccino.

Inside, Lulu introduced me to her friends; one of them was a dark curly-haired young man in a baggy Cecil Gee sweater, the kind coveted by Fulham boys. 'This is Lionel,' she said. 'He writes songs.' Lionel knew everyone. During the next few hours I ligged with Tommy Steele and Wee Willie Harris, an outrageous cross between a circus clown and Bill Haley. Lionel was about to become one of Tin Pan Alley's hot-test properties. He talked and exuded pop. Down the road were the cool jazzers with Gerry Mulligan haircuts, Italian shoes from the Regent shoeshop in Wardour Street, bum-freezer jackets and short raglan-shouldered overcoats. The really cool ones had Vespa scooters. These were to become the notorious Mods.

When Lulu got me back to her room in Meard Street, I promptly passed out on her bed. I was dreaming this beautiful dream, lying in the Greek sunshine, when it started to rain; I could feel it splashing down on me, splashing so hard that it woke me up. I opened my eyes to find that I wasn't on a Greek beach but in a strange little room in Soho, with a man in a camel-hair coat and a spick moustache pissing on me.

'Where's that cow Lulu?' he croaked. 'Now fuck off before I cut your cock off.'

I left very quickly, took a taxi back to Fulham and threw stones at my brother's bedroom window until he let me in.

'Pissed on in Meard Street.' The phrase has stayed with me like a paperback title.

Several months later a Fulham villain called Charley Thomas introduced me to the fine art of gambling, and to his gang of cronies. I knew them because I had sold them ice-cream since I was a kid. They were the big boys. But I was occasionally allowed to hang out with them at the dog-tracks, White City, Stanford Bridge, Wimbledon and Wembley.

The restaurant at White City Dogs had a style all of its own. The major players had regular tables that were always reserved for them. The king gambler was Al Burnett. He owned the Stork Room and the Pigalle, the two hottest night spots in Piccadilly. Resplendent with his camel-hair overcoat and cigar, he had henchmen who would put on his huge bets while he sat at his table drinking champagne with various celebrities. Al tipped us a dog in the fifth race and I put a tenner on it. A tenner was a week's wages – my usual bet was two shillings each way – so it was with mixed feelings that I watched the dogs being loaded into the traps. The lid flew up and the dogs shot out. Our dog won by three lengths at five to one. The table went crazy, and champagne flowed.

After the races I was taken by the big boys to a gambling den. The spieler was run by a Russian Jew who went by the name of Martin Sachs. To my surprise the beautiful Lulu was dealing at the blackjack table. The main game in the room was *chemin de fer*. Charley explained the rules as I wandered about drinking in the atmosphere. Lulu had a break and came and asked me if I was all right. She said that she had been worried about me. I hadn't seen her since I had been pissed on by her Maltese pimp. She looked fantastic in her smart little croupier's cocktail dress. I fell in love all over again. She had to go back to deal and suggested that I give the blackjack a try. An hour later I had won eighty quid. Charley pulled me away and suggested that I put my eighty quid with eighty of his so that we could

24

take a seat at the *chemin de fer* table. This we did, Charley took the seat and I watched him play. It was quite simple, really. If you were dealt an eight or a nine you doubled your money. The real trick seemed to be something they called running a bank. Charley did this a couple of times, which turned our stake into three hundred and fifty quid. 'Your turn,' he said getting up from the table. I sat down, palms sweating. This was a very exciting moment. I took it easy at first, calling a few small bets. Eventually the shoe was passed to me. This meant that I had to put some money in the bank. The last bank had been fifty pounds, so I thought that was the amount that I had to put in. I did, and Charley gave me a funny look. The croupier dealt the cards. The bet was covered and I turned up an ace and an eight. *'Neuf à la banque,'* the croupier cried.

Before I realized what was happening I'd won four tricks in a row, and was staring at eight hundred pounds. Charley whispered in my ear, 'Garage. Garage.' I thought he meant for me to meet him where we had parked his car, so I let the bet ride.

'Fait accompli,' pronounced the croupier.

I turned my cards. The nine and ten of spades looked up at me from the table.

'Sixteen hundred pounds in the bank.'

'Faites les jeux, messieurs et mesdames.'

Charley put his hand on my shoulder and squeezed very hard as he bent down and told me in my ear to take out a thousand pounds and leave six in the bank. By this time a large crowd had gathered around the table. I was seventeen and the centre of attention. Charley leaned down again and whispered, 'Do you feel lucky, son?'

I did feel lucky, and told him so. Charley said, 'Leave it in once more.'

I did, and won. I got up from the table with three thousand two hundred pounds, less the five per cent that the croupier had deducted every time I had won. I proudly carried the chips over to a desk where the manager Martin Sachs sat, his nicotine-stained fingers gripping a cigarette.

'I'll have to give you a cheque,' said Martin in a thick Russian accent. Charley leaned over and said, 'Cash will do, Mr Sachs.'

Mr Sachs patted his pockets and produced various bundles of cash. 'If you prefer, Mr Thomas.'

The Russian walked us to the door and took out a large key with which to let us out. 'Do you mind if I have a word with you. Mim, isn't it? If you know anyone who likes to play cards, bring them along. If they are good punters I will make it worth your while.'

In the car Charley Thomas told me I was a lucky bastard. We shared out our winnings over breakfast in the Jermyn Street Turkish Baths, took some steam and lounged in the oriental atmosphere contemplating our good fortune. Charley dropped me off in the North End Road. I waved as his Jaguar disappeared into the early morning.

It was 5.30 a.m. Just as I was considering the thirty-foot climb up the drainpipe I remembered that the telephone was now in my brother's room. I walked over to Marks & Spencer, where there was a telephone box. Oh. No coins. I picked up the receiver and did what every Fulham lad knew how to do. I tapped out the number on the black Bakelite receiver rest to make a free call. The phone rang twice and a sleepy-voiced Bernard answered.

'It's me. Come down quietly and let me in. I'll be there in two minutes.'

I put down the phone and strolled back to the shop, standing beneath the glow of the giant neon ice-cream cornet that advertised our wares. I heard the lock click. There he was, the little beauty. At that moment I felt a hand on my shoulder. Turning, I saw a uniformed policeman.

'Did you just receive a telephone call from this person?' he said to my kid brother.

'Yes,' said Bernie.

'Good,' said the copper. 'I'm nicking him for stealing electricity, tell your dad we will have him at Fulham Police Station.'

The next morning I appeared at West London Magistrates Court in front of Magistrate Barroclough.

'Read out the charge,' he roared, as grumpy as hell.

My copper piped up, 'Stealing electricity, your honour.'

Barroclough looked at him.

'How much electricity?'

The copper looked embarrassed. 'Tuppence worth, sir.'

Barroclough looked at me. 'Did you, now?' his eyes twinkled.

He looked at my policeman. 'How did he do that?'

The policeman cleared his throat. 'He tapped a telephone call, sir.'

'Did you?' asked the magistrate.

'Yes sir,' I said, hands sweating in the dock. He looked at me over his glasses.

'How did you do that?'

'I tapped it, sir.'

'Show me how you did it,' he said, all nice-like.

I asked the usher for a pencil and showed him. 'One tap for the number one, two taps for the number two and so on, that is unless the number you're dialling has a nought in it, in which case you have to make ten taps for each nought, sir.'

'That's it?' Barroclough picked up a pencil. 'So,' he said, 'if I wish to dial 999, all I have to do is walk into a telephone box, pick up the receiver and tap nine, three times?'

'Yes sir, except 999 calls are free anyway.'

There was a titter in the court. Barroclough looked up and smiled reluctantly.

27

'Well, well. You learn something new every day. I discharge this person on the condition that he pays tuppence over to the arresting officer, who will, I trust, see to it that the cash is returned to its rightful, and I am sure grateful, owner. Case dismissed.'

Chapter Five

By now I was pursuing several different lifestyles. My half-day on Thursdays I usually spent strolling down to South Kensington, where there was a coffee bar called the Mardi Gras opposite the Lycée Français. It was popular with the older students from the Lycée, and the girls were very beautiful. I was, of course, overdressed. I now sported a modified Toby, a fly-away collar and slim-jim tie, and the faithful Jeff Chandler crepes. I soon made friends with a couple of the guys. My best friend at the Mardi Gras was Johnny Gilbert. His father Lewis was a film director; his beautiful mother Hilda liked me and started teaching me some manners. The two hottest chicks in the Mardi Gras were a petite, stunning sixteen-year-old named Edina Ronay and a sexy Trinidadian named Penny Farrar. It soon dawned on Johnny and me that the key to success with women of this calibre was jiving. If you couldn't jive you were nowhere.

Sy Laurie's Jazz Club in Ham Yard was the place. Friday night from seven to midnight we would jive, ringing with sweat, pounding away to live Trad Jazz. As our gang of jivers swelled, the Campbell brothers, Harold Macmillan's two wayward grandsons, joined us in their XK 120 Jags.

For the next year I was a busy boy. The King's Road became my hangout. Coffee bars sprang up: the Sar Ta Torga, the Picasso, the Gilded Cage. The King's Road was happening. The coolest place to hang was the Cozy Café, run by two matronly sisters. We could eat a good lunch at one of their trestle tables for one and sixpence, in the company of workmen, debutantes, gamblers, models, painters and hustlers. I hardly ever slept. Purple Hearts had a lot to do with it. Life was better than good. At the flick of a switch I would change mode and tart up in my new Toby, a horrendous copy of a Savile Row suit, waisted, with a twelve-inch vent at the back, drainpipe trousers and a rose in my button-hole.

I had amassed a couple of grand through gambling and kickbacks from Sachs, and although I showed no sign of this to my family, out on the street at night it was a different kettle of fish. I had become what was known in Fulham as a Jack-the-lad. When I wasn't at the dog-tracks, the Mardi Gras, Sy Laurie's, the King's Road or the ice-cream parlour, I spent time in a plush little drinking club in Knightsbridge.

Dorothy's was a small room above Kutchinsky's, the jewellers, a few doors down from Harrods. Dorothy Foxon was a fantastically gregarious old tart who must have been a stunner in the Thirties. Now in 1958 she was a portly bejewelled creature. There were two watering-holes in Knightsbridge, Dorothy's and Esmeralda's Barn. To these places came the colourful, the crooked and the curious, a fantastic cross-section of London's over- and under-world. At this stage it must be said that I was a very young fringe member, but I made my way easily into the thick of things. The next morning I would be back at my station in the North End Road: 'Yes madam, a threepenny cornet, two sixpenny wafers, and a ninety-nine.'

One hot, sunny day I was tending to an endless queue when a pale blue Ford Thunderbird convertible pulled up to the kerb at the side of the shop. Its driver was the notorious dapper playboy, Dandy Kim. Next to him in the amazing Thunderbird sat Diana Dors. As soon as I saw the car, I dropped my ice-cream spoon and rushed into the parlour proper, leaving my brother Bernie and cousin Gerald at the stainless-steel serving vats to deal with the queue. Inside, I begged my dad to take over for me.

But Dad had a vicious sense of humour: 'No way, get out there and earn your keep.'

I pleaded with him. 'It's Diana Dors come to see me.'

He was making peach melbas for a customer. 'I don't care if it's Princess Margaret, get back out there and get rid of that queue.'

I was mortified. But as Kim and Dorsy entered the shop, to my amazement Dad slid out and took over my station at the vats.

Diana Dors looked fantastic. She was at the height of her powers, she had only just divorced Dennis Hamilton and was yet to marry Dickey Dawson, the comedian, and she was still riding on the success of *A Kid for Two Farthings*. She was the most glamorous film star in England. Within seconds the word had spread up and down the Market that she was in Scala's. It was like the Coronation. The crowds gathered and the shop filled to overflowing. I ushered my celebrity friends onto the high stools in a window seat that looked out over the Market. Dandy Kim introduced me to Diana and ordered two 'Knickerbocker' glories. I went to work and made two spectacular ice-cream sundaes and joined them on the high stools. Mum came down from upstairs with Auntie Tina to help man the pumps. The shop took more money in the next hour than its tills could hold.

I was feeling pretty cool. Dandy Kim was a most sophisticated scoundrel, and Diana Dors, well, what can I say? I was eighteen and impressionable. She was perfect: her platinum blond hair and make-up immaculate; a huge bust, a wasp waist and legs that went on forever. She wore an off-the-shoulder blouse, a tight skirt, white high-heeled shoes and a see-through plastic handbag. She loved the ice-cream sundae. I watched each strawberry as it went into her classic Fifties mouth.

31

Dad came over, unable to resist any longer. 'Aren't you going to introduce me to your friends, then?'

Dad was not to be trusted: his idea of fun at a time like this would be to tell me that the Gaggia needed polishing. 'Meet Fred Scala, the proprietor of this establishment.'

Kim turned on the charm and the wind-up and Dorsy planted a smacker on Dad's shining bald pate, making a perfect impression of her red lips. Dad left it on all day as if he didn't know it was there. Eventually I walked them to the Thunderbird and they drove away through the crowd to let the Market get back to business. Dad and I spent the afternoon with famous lipstick on our foreheads.

Chapter Six

I was having a drink in Dorothy's a few months later and mentioned that I was going to play some cards when Kim and his gang decided to come. We drove off in Dandy Kim's new convertible Rolls to Martin Sachs's spieler. Lord Willoughby, an incredibly rich wastrel who loved a bit of slumming, was in Kim's party. He wore a white linen suit and had Gypsy Rose Lee, the girlfriend of the club-owning gangster Billy Hill, in tow. Cousin Tony, my Uncle Joe and Uncle Petty were at the table. My introduction of the Italians to this game had helped to make it one of the biggest in London. The average bank opened for a couple of hundred pounds and kitties of five grand were not uncommon. I was no longer getting any baksheesh from Sachs, which pissed me off. Later that morning at a club called the Jacaranda Kim remarked, 'It's a pity that Sachs hasn't got any style. His game would be sensational if he had a better front man.' I thought about it and decided to take the plunge.

Moodies was a fantastic stationer's emporium in Bond Street that printed, among other things, all the high-society invitations and calling cards. The gold-leafed paper its craftsmen embossed was second to none. It also customized playing-cards and monogrammed gaming chips.

I went to Moodies, not quite sure of what I was doing. I ordered a set of gaming chips with my initials and monetary denominations on them. The smallest were five pounds, escalating up to lovely dark-blue plaques with '£5000' printed on them in gold. Three weeks later I collected them in their green baize-lined tin box. They cost me three hundred pounds. I took them home and in the secrecy of my bedroom played out imaginary games of *chemin de fer*.

In another Moodies box there were also one thousand 'Mim Scala At-Home' invitation cards, beautifully embossed with the address and date left blank. Although gaming was illegal, there was, of course, a loophole. As long as each game took place in a different establishment, it could assume the status of a private party.

By day I still worked for my dad, at night I was whizzing all over London, to the dog-tracks, the Turkish baths, the drinking clubs. I would give one of my cards to any suitable gambler that I came across.

My first *soirée* took place in a house in Pont Street, occupied by a lanky, amusing, terribly broke Old Etonian by the name of Tommy Jebb. Tommy had agreed that for one hundred pounds in cash I could have the use of his house for one night. As I travelled about inviting people, I told them that the game was going to be huge and that the Italians would be coming. I had also told Cousin Tony and Uncle Petty that the game would be huge and that Lord Willoughby and a load of aristocrats would be there. This was how I promoted the event. My next mission was to acquire two tables. Harrods provided two beautiful tables worth one hundred and fifty pounds each. I hired a young croupier called Andrew Simpson and he produced another public-school charmer by the name of Bob Hyder to be my second man. I got hold of Lulu, who was by now a very good friend. She would deal the blackjack. As the big day drew near I made final arrangements, buying the drink, renting a few dozen glasses, and personally preparing trays full of little sandwiches in Tommy Jebb's kitchen. Tommy had got into the spirit of the thing and for an extra tenner agreed to be the butler. I then took a taxi to the North End Road where Mr Tobias was finishing the last buttonhole on my new tuxedo.

Ten o'clock. Andrew, Bob, Lulu and Tommy waited with me for the doorbell to ring. I felt like Rick in *Casablanca*, my tin box of Moodies gaming chips at the ready. The plan was that Andrew and Bob would run the game and drop five per cent of every winning bet down the caniot slot in the table. There was a drawer under this slot which I hoped to empty regularly. Eleven o'clock came and a cocktail party was in progress, populated by friends and acquaintances from Chelsea, but there was not one punter amongst them. I had invested a grand in this venture, and a grand was all I had, apart from the wages my dad was paying me, but I consoled myself with the fact that the party was good anyway. The house was full of characters from the Chelsea set: the girls were all pretty, mostly debutantes, as well as Anthony Hayden-Guest, Nicholas Simonack, Mark Sykes, Michael Beeby, Henrietta Tiarks, Lord Valentine Thynne and his stepsisters Sabrina and Georgia Tennant. But no gamblers.

Twelve o'clock, and things were getting edgy. The booze had run out, the sandwiches had been scoffed and quite suddenly everyone left to go to the Jacaranda. I did not feel well. Tommy felt very well; he had drunk several bottles of cheap champagne and only by withholding his payment did I persuade him to hang around. Lulu was being chatted up by Lord Valentine. Andrew and Bob were still with me for the same reason as Tommy.

Then the bell rang and Tommy answered it as taxis began pulling up outside. The Italians had arrived, and Lord Willoughby and a party of loonies from Soho rolled in noisily. Dorothy Foxon came with a cab full of her friends: Jo Deagle and his partner Pauline Wallace, Lucian Freud and Francis Bacon, with Muriel from her drinking club in Soho. Kim and Dorsy arrived with Andrew Rae, star of *The Yellow Balloon*. I was behind my desk dishing out chips. Dorothy felt sorry for me and had sent her famously gay barman Aubrey back to the club for a taxiful of booze.

My casino was happening. Freud and Bacon were lunatic punters. Lucian was a weird-looking man, pale, thin, with bright, dancing eyes and a mop of unruly curls. He had a nervous twitch, beautiful hands, and used safety-pins for cuff-links. His companion on the night was a young, scar-faced pretty boy from Soho.

Lord Willoughby was outrageous, tall in a white linen suit, as affected as a dancing master. He had a habit of dribbling in his pants and would wear a foppish silk handkerchief hanging from his belt to cover the offending stain. The Italians were delighted to be in such illustrious company. The bell never stopped ringing, and the chips kept dropping down into the caniot slot. Both tables punted into the morning: six o'clock, seven o'clock, eight o'clock. I had to be back in the North End Road at nine to open the shop. The game was peaking but had enough life in it to churn through until midday. I persuaded Cousin Tony to call my dad and tell him that I was with him in the country and that the car had broken down. Dad grumbled but accepted the fib. I had several thousand pounds in cash in the drawer of my desk, plus cheques from Lord Willoughby, Lucian, and several other punters whom I knew to be good for their losses. Mercifully it was Ascot week. The hard core finally left bleary-eyed to get changed for the races. As I cashed in the chips for the last guest, it dawned on me that all the money in the desk was now mine: three and a half grand, including the cheques. I gave Andrew and Bob a hundred each, and stuffed two hundred in the sleeping Tommy's pocket with a note apologizing for the mess. I slipped Lulu twenty-five and left.

Cousin Tony, an old hand at all-night gambling, was impressed with my takings and wanted to join me in the venture; that way he could guarantee that the Italians would turn up for the next game. So he and my Uncle Joe and

36

Uncle Petty became my partners. I hid my money box behind several hundred boxes of ice-cream cornets in the storeroom and carried on as usual. Dad never said a word, but as the games went on he began to smell a rat. For one thing my accent was changing, and he used to give me dodgy looks when he caught me putting on my 'Next, please, wafers or cornets?' voice instead of, ''Ow menny, love? Wayfers owr cornits?' Well, I had to start somewhere.

An individual called Gaston de Chalus took over from Tommy as the greeter. As the weeks passed I noticed that a few very unsavoury punters had infiltrated the game. About two in the morning, a game was in full swing. I was enjoying myself as usual, wandering about having the odd bet and watching the five per cent caniot drop down the house slot when Gaston came over with two well-dressed punters he had just let in.

I shook hands with the two men in light brown herring-bone suits, obviously twins. One of them produced a grand in cash and asked for some chips. I was delighted to oblige. They seemed all right. It appeared they knew Lucian Freud and Dandy Kim and Tim Willoughby, so I thought no more of it.

I continued to enjoy the game. The twins lost their money in a civilized fashion and strolled over to me.

'Can we have a word with you in private?' They followed me into one of the bedrooms. We were in a studio house in Kinnerton Street.

'Nice house,' said one of the twins.

'Yeah, it's not bad,' said I naïvely.

'Nice game,' said the other twin.

'Thank you,' I said with a bit of pride.

'It's a pity you don't like our game.' They stared at me.

'You run a game, do you?' I asked innocently.

'You know we fucking run a game and you have been putting it about that it's bent. That's bad for our business.'

'I'm sorry,' I said. 'I don't know you, I know nothing about your game and if I did I certainly wouldn't criticize it. Every man for himself and all that.'

The twins looked at me. It was a menacing look, an East End look, a cockney cock-of-the-walk look.

'I tell you what we are going to do,' said one of them. 'We are going to let it go this time.'

The other one grinned at me. I knew that grin as well.

'Now if we hear on the grapevine that you're slagging us off, we will be back. And we'll probably break both your legs.'

With that, they turned and walked back to the game. They got to the door, had a few words with Gaston, and turned to me. 'Nice game, we really enjoyed ourselves.'

The door closed. I was in shock. I called Gaston aside. Gaston had a very prominent nose and adenoid problems, which caused him to twitch his nose and sniff. He had turned this habit into an affectation.

'What do you think you are doing, letting characters like that in to the game? Who the fuck are they, they just threatened to break my legs,' I stammered, all furious and indignant.

I soon found out that the Kray twins ran the West End, and that they killed people.

Over the next few days I made some enquiries. I then talked to Cousin Tony. We decided to carry on. At the next game three hoods in balaclava helmets rushed past Gaston, smashed the house up and left.

The whole thing was getting too heavy. I had a nice little stash behind the ice-cream cones in the parlour basement, and I had a major crush to pursue.

Chapter Seven

Sabrina Tennant, the most beautiful girl in Chelsea, had invited me to spend a weekend in the country with her mother and stepfather, the Marchioness and Marquis of Bath, Virginia and Henry, in Job's Mill on their estate at Longleat in Wiltshire. She was seventeen and just a little fascinated with this cockney boy from the North End Road, who was very fascinated by her.

We were greeted by Sabrina's mother, a staggeringly handsome woman, who pushed the latest addition to the Thynne family in an ancient pram. A tall, thin gentleman in a threadbare tweed jacket with frayed cuffs strode out of the house, extending his hand.

'Henry. You must be Vim.'

'Mim,' I said, 'with an M.'

'Yes, quite, Vim, come on in.' They were charming and showed no sign of disappointment at their daughter's choice of house guest. We spent the day wandering about the estate. During the afternoon Henry announced that it was time for a swim. In Fulham it wasn't usual to strip off in front of strangers, so with much embarrassment I joined the family for a naked dip in the mill-race. Sabrina was not just beautiful, she was excitingly weird. Naturally I presumed that she was in love with me – a very foolish thing to do, given her similar fascination for several of my King's Road contemporaries.

The following week she departed with her sister Georgia for

Spain. I was heartbroken, but received a sort of vague invitation to come on down to Torremolinos.

Back in the North End Road the strain of trying to maintain my various lifestyles was beginning to take its toll. I counted out my gambling proceeds. I had three grand in cash and another two or so in bounced cheques.

My friends who worked in the Market, Alfie Frost, the Johnson brothers, Terry Priddle and the Watts brothers, were all off on their annual holiday to Southend. I told Mum and Dad that I was going with them. I was entitled to a holiday, so they did not object. However, I had other plans.

With a passport and a cash stash, I bought a ticket on the Golden Arrow. I was dressed in my best Prince of Wales suit and smart shoes, sitting in a first-class carriage with bundles of money in my dodgy suitcase. The splendid Golden Arrow, one of the last great English trains, chugged at high speed to Dover. Crossing the channel was a very civilized affair. Once in France the Golden Arrow puffed and steamed its way to Paris. I climbed out at the Gare St-Lazare. This was my first foreign journey, and like a novice traveller I wandered around the vicinity of the station looking for the action that Paris was famous for, and checked my bag into a cheap hotel.

My first impressions of Paris were not good. Drinking beer in the back streets of St-Lazare in the company of drab Parisian workmen was not what I expected. I would be having much more fun in Southend with the boys. How was I to know that half a mile away the real Paris awaited? I became adventurous, and took a long walk to the Arc de Triomphe and the boulevards St-Germain and St-Michel. I spoke no French and nobody made the slightest effort to talk to me. I strolled up and down the boulevards feeling very lonely. This foreign travel was not all it was cracked up to be.

I wandered until I found myself in Les Halles. It reminded me of Soho, and the North End Road, with characters drinking in the pavement cafés, hipsters and bohemians. For the first couple of days I cut no ice. I thought my Prince of Wales suit had something to do with it, so in a flea market I bought my first pair of button-up 501s, a *blouson noir* and a pair of Spanish working boots, rushed back to the room in my new residence, the Hotel des Beaux Arts, and changed.

I hit the street and waited for a beautiful long-haired black-eyed French girl to come and sit next to me. A good-looking American guy in blue jeans and a Sloppy Joe T-shirt sat next to me instead. He offered to take me to some of the more interesting places. We started a bar crawl. I wasn't flashing my money about, but I did buy drinks and dinner, after which he invited me to visit some of his friends. We climbed several hundred steps to the top floor of a large dilapidated house. In the apartment, half a dozen guys were fucking each other on the carpet. A fat one jumped up, pink and naked, flung his arms around my friend, and squealed with delight. I stood there transfixed until he tried to stroke my balls. I chinned him for not asking permission, split my knuckles on his teeth, and sprinted down the stairwell four steps at a time.

Back on the street I resumed my search for the good life.

The Blue Note was just a door in a wall but had the sweetest music I had ever heard wafting through it. Inside, a four-piece band were busy nursing a groove. The leader, sweat-covered, handsome and cool, was playing his trumpet to a full house of jazz aficionados. This was it, the real thing at last.

I sat at a table and met Justine. She had nowhere to stay. Soon I had fallen in love again and she moved her travelling bag into my hotel. She told me that she had been in Paris for six months looking for work as a dancer. We cruised the jazz clubs and restaurants of Paris. She took me to parties and taught me how to make love. She woke me in the mornings with a fresh baguette and coffee. On the fourth or fifth morning Justine announced that she had to go home to Marseilles. Her

41

mother was ill and she needed money for the hospital. I brought her to the station and gave her a couple of hundred pounds.

I sulked about for a day or two, wandering around, exploring St-Germain. I took a seat in an outdoor café and ordered an absinthe with a café noir on the side. I was beginning to get the hang of the place. Suddenly Justine came out of the crowd on the arm of a tall, handsome black man. She passed my table, saw me, and looked right through me. I had never been hustled before. I was choked.

Chapter Eight

I checked out of my hotel and caught the wagon-lit to Malaga. An American kid on the train gave me a book, Jack Kerouac's *On the Road*. I read it as the train took me across the Pyrenees. It was the first book I had read since leaving school, and it blew me away.

I was on the road. Fifty miles up the coast was the beautiful Sabrina. The Torremolinos bus was packed with Spanish country folk and their chickens. The air was garlic-flavoured and unbearably hot. With great difficulty I persuaded the driver to let me keep my suitcase with me; he wanted to tie it on the roof with the livestock and boxes of farm equipment. The journey started uncomfortably and got progressively worse. About a mile out of Malaga the road became a dirt track. The bus swayed on its overloaded springs around precarious bends, and a dust cloud enveloped us for the whole journey. We passed through the pueblo of Mijas and the pretty little fishing village of Fuengirola. By this time I was dying of thirst. A fellow passenger noticed my plight and kindly offered me a drink from his leather bottle from which he expertly squirted what looked a thirst-quenching stream of ruby-coloured liquid. I raised it and squeezed. A hot jet of the bitter wine shot into my eyes, down my face, and finally into my mouth. I steadied my aim and drank half a pint of the stuff. The journey immediately improved; the strong wine went straight to my head. At the next stop we refilled the leather bottle in a sweltering bus-station *tienda*, my Spanish saviour grinning at the effect that his gift had had on me.

I eventually tumbled off the bus in a dusty little square. There were only two streets in Torremolinos. One ran from the beach to the hills at the back of the town and the other, which I had come in on, crossed the village as part of the coast road. Where these two roads crossed was the village square. There were four bars, a post office, a nightclub called the Whisky-a-Go-Go and a few shops. In the surrounding hills I could see a few well-spaced villas. There were of course other buildings in the town but I hardly noticed them. They were the colour of the earth. Plastic signs and neon had not reached the Costa del Sol. I found a *pensione*, paid a week's rent, and happily lay down on the thin mattress to sleep. I was awoken by the sound of flamenco guitars, bongos and raucous voices. I looked out from my balcony to see a gaggle of young people armed with instruments, beach blankets and bottles of wine in procession down the steps heading for the beach, and someone from the balcony beneath mine was shouting at them.

I showered, left my room and followed, soon finding myself in the midst of a crowd of sun-tanned revellers.

'Hello Mim! Welcome to Torremolinos. When did you arrive?' It was Paco, one of the more colourful waiters from the Picasso, a favourite Chelsea hangout. Paco passed me a hand-rolled cigarette.

'Smoke some of this. I just came back from Tangiers.'

I smoked the offering, my first joint. The flames grew higher, the music sounded better and the night sky twinkled with stars. I lay on my back feeling wonderful. I tried to get up but spun out hopelessly, so I gave in to the intoxication and lay there, eyes closed, flattened against the sand and hoping desperately not to fall off the earth.

'This is Mim, he's a gambler from London.'

I pulled myself together, pushing myself up on my elbows.

There was Sabrina, as beautiful as ever, standing next to a good-looking young man in dirty white sailor's trousers. They were both soaking wet. He had his arm around her and she didn't seem to mind.

'When did you arrive?'

I made some incomprehensible reply and was promptly sick.

The days passed in a blissful haze of drink, sun and marijuana. I reckoned I was now a practising dharma bum, a beatnik, a very cool guy. There was a nightclub in the village square called La Fiesta. Chantal, a French bohemian beauty, sang moody songs with her guitar at midnight. She was a perfect dharma partner. She lived in an attic, wore no shoes, had long, jet-black hair that flowed down her back like oil, and she sang like a bird. She was also on the game, but I didn't know this until I caught my first dose of the clap. The American doctor who treated me with the antibiotic needle asked if I was sleeping with Chantal.

'That makes about two hundred of us,' he said. 'Take these and don't drink for a week.'

As the summer hotted up, the long-term residents started to give really good parties. David Tennant arrived on the scene. Sabrina and I were good friends at this point and hung out in a loose gang of young English kids that included Michael and Jane Rainey. One day she invited me to Ronda with her dad and some friends. Several cars lined up to take the Tennant guests on the adventure. I found myself in a car with Sabrina and her cousin, the notorious and extremely beautiful Suna Portman. In the group was a drunk writer called Ernest and a French singer-actress called Juliette. We drank wine from leather bottles as the procession of cars took the scenic route through Andalucia up into the mountains towards the Romano-Moorish splendour of Ronda. We arrived at midday to the buzz of the town's Goyesca – a celebration of the famous painter. Hundreds of young men in costume rode beautiful horses

45

through the town, and beside them rode women with their hair piled high on tortoise-shell combs, fans of lace hovering in front of their faces as in Goya's paintings. Our procession crossed the ancient Roman bridge spanning the gorge that led into the town. Heraldic flags fluttered in the breeze.

Ernest and the men headed directly to the bar of the Grand Hotel while the women went off alone. We drank tequila with fresh orange juice; we drank it neat with salt and lemon; and then we drank it with coffee so that we could sober up for the bullfight.

The Plaza de Torros in Ronda is the oldest bullring in Spain. Stone columns surrounded the corrida and above these were the private boxes. The place was packed and trumpets sounded for the procession to begin. The beautiful young women of Ronda and their men rode fiery horses in the blinding sunshine reflected from the immaculate sand. The trumpets sounded again and into the ring came the armoured picadors, their horses moving strangely under the weight of the padded heraldic mattresses that hung from their sides. Then, on foot, came the dazzling matadors; young and agile and cocky, they swaggered across the sand.

When the stars entered the ring, the crowd went wild: Antonio Ordoñez, Spain's current favourite, was followed by his arch-rival Miguel Domingine. They had been fighting a series of *mano-a-mano* confrontations throughout the year. (Hemingway would publish his account of their duels, 'The Dangerous Summer', in 1960.)

The atmosphere in our box was electric. Suna, Sabrina and David Tennant, the Rainey family and I settled down as a hush came over the crowd. From a side-door rode the splendid figure of one of the *rejoneadores*, the flanks of his horse gleaming in the sunlight. He cantered to the centre of the sand circle. A man who looked like Sancho Panza slid back the bolt on a dark oak door, revealing a black tunnel. The bull appeared from

46

the darkness at a trot, head and horns high, sniffed the air, swung his handsome head and charged the lone horseman. The rider moved his horse in tight circles using his knees as the furious bull attempted in vain to lift both horse and rider into the sky. Occasionally the horse would break into a gallop, encouraging the bull to give chase. The bull swung wildly as two darts penetrated the muscle at the base of its neck. I remember being mesmerized at the combination of the grace and ease of the horse and rider and the power and fury of the bull. The rider galloped to the side of the ring and picked up a sword. The bull snorted in the centre of the lonely disc of sand, tired and angry. The *rejoneador* circled a while, then rode in to plunge the sword between the horns. The bull was on its side twitching, with blood gushing from its nostrils. The Sancho Panza figure ran to it and, with a deft push with a short, wide blade, severed the animal's spinal cord. It twitched twice and was dead. The applause for the rider and the bull was extraordinary; young women and men alike were caught in the blood-lust and the glory of killing and dying.

Antonio Ordoñez had drawn a huge bull. It entered the ring from the black tunnel at a gallop, charging the *barrera*, and hooking the top two planks off one of the retreating barriers. This pleased the crowd immediately. Even after the picadors had lanced the neck muscles two or three times, and five *banderilas* dangled from its hump, it still did not slow down. Ordoñez faced his opponent. He swirled, each pass bringing a roar from the crowd until the ritual dance was over. The bull was dead. I have stood in the stands at Wembley Stadium for Cup Finals, but the sound of the crowd in the Ronda bullring that day will stay with me to the grave.

Ordoñez was awarded two ears and the tail for his first bull of the day. He strutted around the *barrera* as flowers, hats, and seat cushions showered onto the sand. First, he threw his hat into the president's box, then, as the crowd screamed, he threw the tail high into the crowd. A feverish host of hands clutched as he threw up an ear. Under our box, he threw the other ear into the air, and a black silky object with a bloody stump fell out of a bright blue sky into my hand. Everyone in the box went crazy, chanting 'bravo, bravo!' I offered the ear to a beautiful woman in the group whom I'd noticed earlier. She graciously declined. 'You keep it, Mim, to remember this day.'

I kept it for years, pickled in a jar of *Hinebra secca*, until my mother found it ('that horrible thing') at home and threw it away.

Chapter Nine

Quite suddenly I was bored, in need of an adventure. One of us, Simon, suggested Morocco and off we went on his BSA, crossing from Spain to North Africa by ferry. The streets of Tangiers were lined with expensive cars. In the harbour, luxury yachts bobbed about next to each other, each with a separate party going on board. We parked the bike outside the Café de Paris and took a table. I hadn't even sipped my coffee when I heard my name.

'Mim! 'Ow are ya son? What you doing 'ere?'

It was Charley James, a London gambler of dubious character. He was all dolled up in a tropical suit while we dharma bums sported Levis and Moroccan shirts.

'Still gambling are you, Mim?'

'Not for a while, Charley. I took a holiday.'

Charley gave me a funny look. 'Well, you're in luck. Billy Hill is giving a party tonight. You remember Billy, don't you? He came to a couple of your games with me.'

Simon listened to the conversation in bewilderment. Billy Hill was a celebrated English gangster. Simon and I checked into the Atlas Hotel, cleaned ourselves up and made our way to the address that Charley had given me. It was on Marchand, the only big boulevard in Tangiers, where the rich lived, their gardens overlooking the Straits of Gibraltar. The first person to greet me was a swarthy man wearing an immaculate white turban with a ruby in it. I introduced Simon to Charles de

Silva, one-time dishwasher in an Indian restaurant, now one of the world's finest confidence tricksters with a permanent suite at the Ritz. Next came Lord Willoughby, who had knocked me with a wrongly dated cheque for twelve hundred quid just before I left London. I might have been in Knightsbridge instead of Tangiers. Billy Hill had taken over from Jack Spot and Albert Dimes, who had lost control of the West End after their public, and bloody, knife fight on the corner of Old Compton Street, which made the front pages of every newspaper in London.

Gambling was in progress. Before I knew it I had lost fifteen hundred quid in traveller's cheques chasing a bank at a chemmie table. The next day Simon and I caught the ferry back to Spain. I stayed in Torremolinos just long enough to collect the envelope with the rest of my traveller's cheques from the safe at Sandy's Bar and took the bus back to Algeciras and the ferry to Tangiers. There was no point in hanging about, I wanted to get my money back. In Tangiers I checked into the Minza, a lovely old hotel. At seven o'clock I hit the bar. There they were, the chaps, de Silva, Paddy, the amazingly drunk eccentric landlord of the notorious Star Tavern in Belgrave Mews, and a host of the leading lights of London's underworld. With them were Lord Willoughby and Barbara Hutton, the Woolworth's heiress, and a bunch of international celebrities. Tim Willoughby was civil; he acknowledged what he owed me, and I was relieved to hear it. I hit the tables knowing that if I did lose, I'd still have substantial funds to fall back on. Soon I had lost almost everything. I had two hundred pounds left. Embarrassed, I lay low, exploring the seedier side of Tangiers.

The city was full of surprises. I found the Petit Socco and the kif cafés. While enjoying a smoke in the Café Baba, I came across a gang of hip and crazy Americans. One of them had a trumpet he took everywhere, blowing cool jazz riffs whenever he felt like it. Another claimed to be a poet, on his way back from a convention in Paris. Quite suddenly I really was a dharma bum.

My new companions were the real ones, the Beat Generation in Tangiers for some R&R. I had only just started smoking grass but they had drugs: heroin. Their mentor was a strange individual, William Burroughs. Naturally I had to try a bit of heroin. Suddenly I knew what they meant. I soon out-dharma'd the dharmas by blowing nearly two grand in a few days. Crazy man, crazy.

I bade farewell to Tangiers and travelled back to Spain to look for Lord Willoughby in Torremolinos, and my money. He never showed up. I was left penniless. Some time later he took off in a speedboat and was never seen again. Lord Willoughby de Eresby's obituary in *Who's Who* reads: 'Reported missing at sea.'

I didn't want to stay in Torremolinos. I was also in need of more heroin, but there were no junkies in Torremolinos so I just felt bad and tried to forget about it. The cavalry arrived in the shape of two very nice young English boys. We decided to try to get back to England by walking across Spain. I spoke a bit of Spanish by now and they liked me. I was completely broke. The three of us set off to walk to Bilbao. We got as far as Granada. What a journey we had, walking over the mountains of the Sierra Nevada, befriended by a family of gypsies in the caves of Sacramonte. We hung out for a couple of weeks listening to the real flamenco and living the real life until they too ran out of money. Martin, one of the boys, cabled his dad who came up with three train tickets to London. I had only been doing heroin for a short time, and soon learned that without it I felt awful. I reached London tired and strung out. Where would I go? The number 11 bus made up my mind for me. It went to the North End Road. On 12 September 1959, I walked back into Scala's Ice-Cream Parlour.

Chapter Ten

London had subconsciously been preparing for the Sixties while I had been away. Although few people knew it as yet, the few square miles of Fulham and Chelsea were soon to become the centre of the universe for my generation. I sheepishly appeared in my dad's ice-cream parlour, not knowing what sort of reception to expect. He spotted me, and his face momentarily lit up.

'Hello, son, get your coat on, and help your brother out. Can't you see he's got a queue?' The coat he referred to was the white jacket of the ice-cream man. I obeyed. Nothing had changed; it was like riding a bike.

'Move over, bro.' I took my place at one of the vats. 'Yes, miss, two wafers and a cornet.'

The King's Road set welcomed me back like a hero. My journey had done my street credibility a power of good, but back on a tenner a week I could no longer be Jack-the-lad.

There were now several *chemin de fer* games going on, all vying for the same bunch of punters. But the scene had lost its charm. I couldn't have got back into it even if I had wanted to. Besides, the law was about to change. Betting had been legalized, betting shops opened, and casinos were being granted licences.

Cousin Tony was running Esmeralda's Barn as a casino, and it had somehow become the West End headquarters of the Kray twins. As always there was a dark side to the Chelsea set. The hard-core aristocrats – Mark Sykes, Valentine and Christopher Thynne, Suna and Mickey Portman – were still around. This action was supplemented by the steady influx of country gentry, mostly rich and easy targets. All social barriers had been let down. For the first time since the days of the Regency bucks, the riff-raff and the aristocracy mingled freely. Etonians acquired strange cockney accents, and cockneys spoke posh.

I wasn't the only cockney moving around in this shuffled deck of humanity. It had become completely credible for well-bred young girls to have naughty King's Road boyfriends. The central meeting-place on the King's Road was the Markham pub. Just a few yards to the south was the Temperance Billiard Hall (now the Chelsea Antique Market). More coffee bars had sprung up. The Kenco was buzzing at the Sloane Square end. The Cozy Café was in the middle. Several notorious beatniks dominated the scene. John Fenton the Jazzer knew the matrix number of every jazz record in Dobells off by heart. Michael Beeby, a tall and handsome charmer from Guildford, had grabbed himself Miss Henrietta Tiarks. Johnny Somers, Irish and moody, was one of the best pullers on the road. Tommy Waldron, a.k.a. Cholmondeley, and Alan Travers-Brown, were scallywags adored by all manner of women. Bobby Buckley, a pretty leprechaun of an Irish boy with a slight stammer but as hard as nails, was soon to become Reggie Kray's best friend. Naturally I left the ice-cream dream once more.

This cast of characters, including myself, all had one thing in common: no visible means of support. We all lived by our wits, one moment famine, the next a feast. Pocket money was mostly acquired by hustling snooker at the Temperance, or utilizing the football machine in the Markham. Somehow all major social events were attended. Great skill was required to cop an invite to events like Henley or Ascot, and only super cunning could get you in to the big debutante balls at Grosvenor House or the Dorchester, or the private ones in the country. A ball wasn't considered a ball if the King's Road set were not in attendance, diligently hustling their stiffies. If the required invitations were not forthcoming by the night of the event, it was quite acceptable to gatecrash, provided that the manner of entry was outrageous enough.

The London season of 1959 was probably the peak of these extravagant coming-out balls. Paul Tanfield of the *Daily Mail* and his assistant Nigel Dempster kept the public informed of our exploits. If anything exciting happened, they printed it. Cholmondeley would think nothing of entering the Hyde Park Hotel via the laundry chute, with a glass in one pocket and a bottle of Babycham in the other. Once in, he would fill his glass and wander lost until he was in the heart of the party.

One summer night, the Kray twins were debating Bobby Buckley's prowess as a boxer at the bar of Esmeralda's Barn. Cholmondeley, being broke, offered to fight Bobby for fifty pounds, and Reggie Kray took the bet. If Cholmondeley hurt Bobby or marked his pretty face, Mr Kray might be very upset; on the other hand, if Cholmondeley lost, he would not be able to pay the honourable gangster. A makeshift ring was set up on the dance floor. At two in the morning the fight began, watched by a full house including Lord Boothby, Ronnie Kray's political chum. I acted as Cholmondeley's second.

Bobby boxed my man around the ring for two rounds. Cholmondeley took punch after punch on the chin without going down. The place was a madhouse, with cheering and shouting from the Krays and their gang of attendants. Cholmondeley could not land a punch. At the third bell I told him he was not winning, and he suggested we might have to do a runner. The bell went for the last round. Bobby came dancing in. Cholmondeley took three mighty clouts to the head but stood there like a bull. Then, from nowhere, he threw a direct hit to Bobby's nose. Blood spurted from his nostrils. He didn't go down and was quite ready to finish the fight, but the sight of blood was too much for Ronnie Kray. He threw fifty pounds into the ring, jumped in and stopped the fight.

'I'm all right, I'm all right,' shouted Bobby.

'No, you ain't, son. You used to be much prettier than you are now. Now you can all fuck off home.'

Cholmondeley and I did as we were told, fifty quid the richer.

A couple of days later I was in the billiard hall with Cholmondeley and some other gamblers studying form. We were just winning a few quid when Two-Moon Tom (so called because he was always getting two-month stretches in the Scrubs for petty larceny) came in announcing a tip for a dog at the afternoon meeting at Park Royal, so we broke off and strolled down to the Cozy for a spot of lunch.

Seated in a booth opposite was a most beautiful red-head whom I recognized from the hundreds of giant milk advertisements at that time decorating every available billboard in London. Her name was Cindy Cassidy, a top model with the Lucy Clayton Agency. Torn between Park Royal and Cindy, I settled for the dog, but not before offering to take Cindy to the première of *Ben Hur*.

Park Royal was crowded for an afternoon meeting. We blagged our way into the directors' stand, keeping a pound of our stake for train fare, and punted all our cash on Two-Moon Tom's tip. Naturally the dog got baulked at the first bend and lost. We debated how long it would take us to walk back to Chelsea, and put all our train fare on forecasts with the next favourite. Bang! Up comes six and two. We had the forecast twice and stood to collect about a fiver. I fed the ticket through the payout grille to the little blue-rinsed lady inside. She did a bit of arithmetic and started to count out money.

'Two hundred and twenty-two pounds.'

She looked at me with a smile and slid the heap across. I

picked it up in shock. Bookie's tellers were always right. I walked over to Cholmondeley, gave him a nod and he followed me out. Overcome with our good fortune, we slid into a pub and split the booty. I telephoned Johnny Gilbert, and he had failed to get me the *Ben Hur* tickets, so instead we spent eighty pounds on a Vespa from a showroom on Willesden High Street and drove to Cindy Cassidy's address in Hans Crescent. Cindy came out looking like a red-haired Doris Day, in a white taffeta evening-dress with shoes of the same material. Ginny Strevens, another Lucy Clayton model, followed behind, inspecting Cindy's date.

Cholmondeley and I disowned the Vespa and hailed a cab as Cholmondeley invited Ginny to join the party. After an uncomfortable ten minutes in the cab, Cindy suggested that it was going the wrong way for Leicester Square and the *Ben Hur* première. I changed the subject until the cab stopped at the restaurant entrance of the White City dog-track, where we had a reservation. I bunged the *maitre d'* a fiver, and he glided us to a table.

The two girls made for a stunning entrance. A bottle of champagne and a few oysters later, Cindy had forgiven me for the deception and we were ready for the first race. Halfway through the evening Al Burnett, the legendary gambler and nightclub owner, sent one of his men to invite us for a drink. We accepted, joining the power table.

After a drink or two he leaned across. 'Didn't I see you at Park Royal this afternoon?'

I got a bit edgy. 'Yes.'

'Did you have a little tickle in the seventh race? About two hundred quid's worth of a tickle?'

He gazed at me, I looked at Cholmondeley, then he laughed.

'That was my money; she paid you by mistake.' After an uncomfortable pause, he continued. 'It's okay, you're off the hook; she paid me out again. My man put my winning tickets on

Grakle, winner of the 1931 Grand National at Liverpool's Aintree racecourse, with jockey Bob Lyall aboard and trainer Tom Coulthwaite in the foreground.

Geofredo Scala, Auntie Virginia, Auntie Millie with her husband Uncle Joe, and lucky Emilio in the newly opened ice-ceam parlour in the North End Road, Fulham.

The Scala home, Hamilton Lodge, in Honour Oak Road, Forest Hill, south-east London, 1938. (*Gerald Mancini*)

Geofredo Scala, *lower left*, leads his squad (the Royal Electrical and Mechanical Engineers) out of Aldershot en route to Burma, May 1943.

Above Geofredo and Angelina Scala leave Southwark Cathedral, London, after their wedding, 19 February 1939.

Above right Uncle Joe, dressed to kill, 1939.

Below Bernard and Mim in Granddad's chair at Hamilton Lodge, 1947. (*Gerald Mancini*)

Right Geofredo Scala with his trusty cue, after winning the Taylor Walker London Billiards Championship, 1951.

Howard Bond, Mim, and Jonesie, three budding artists at St Edmund's Secondary Modern Schoool, Hammersmith, 1955.

A typical afternoon outside Scala's Ice Creamery in Fulham's North End Road Market during the mid 1950s. (*Gerald Mancini*)

her counter and stepped away to look at the Tote board. When he came back you'd been paid out and had scarpered. I'm very well known at Park Royal, so I had a huge row. Eventually I got paid out as well. I wouldn't go back there too soon if I were you, though. Now go on and buy us all a drink.'

Chapter Eleven

Having flown the nest for the romance of the King's Road, I had given no serious thought to the prospect of gainful employment. A kind of hedonistic abandon began to prevail as the Sixties set in. There was no need to get a job. Apart from the thirty bob a week for my Tite Street bedsit I had no need of a regular wage. I had become extremely proficient at table football and could always hustle a bob or two in the Markham or at the snooker hall, but any time I did fall upon a few quid it seemed to vanish quickly at a dog-track.

At this time Ronan O'Rahilly was scrabbling around for something King's-Roady to do. Ronan and Michael Joseph, a studious young Stanislavsky fan, opened a King's Road version of the Actors' Workshop.

I became very interested in this project. The Workshop operated from a studio flat in the old Chelsea village which I was to move into. My studio consisted of one large room, a loo and a bathroom. The furnishings consisted of some floor-to-ceiling Donegal tweed drapes on the windows, and several milk crates with old doors resting on them as coffee-tables. Thus the Chelsea Actors' Workshop was formed.

The actual classes were based on those at the Actors' Workshop in New York. Cassavetes, Monroe, Brando, Dean and McQueen were the warriors of the acting profession. Terry Stamp and Julie Christie turned up for the odd class. The most outstanding student, however, was a pert little girl with doe eyes, Georgina Hale. Somehow Ronan raised enough cash to make a movie, *High Heels*, which was to star Georgina and employ the whole of the Workshop. So we all got unpaid jobs on the production, which was all very well until union problems stopped the production. But, for some of us, our blood was up. We wanted to make movies. Together with two students of the Workshop, Johnny Somers and an American, Dan Eggink, we drove over to Ireland in a rented Buick, with a tripod, an Ariflex 35mm camera and a bootful of film. We acted, directed and produced our first film disaster.

It was 1960. I had now officially left home, I had no money and no job, and was sharing a house at 29 Tite Street with Norman Thaddeus Vane, writer and heir to an American ice-cream fortune, Michael Ross, who was painting large mad canvases (and eventually became a rock and roll manager), Cindy Cassidy, and other itinerants. I was back hustling a living at snooker. We would play a game for the price of the table and a pound. If you won, you had the price of lunch in the Cozy Café; if you lost you paid or got beaten up.

There were some great characters at the Temperance, the charismatic gang including the Faginesque David Litvinoff, the asthmatic, waif-like Eddie Dylan and the moody artist Brian Masset. One of these guys had a secret life when he was not hanging around the Temperance. Litvinoff engaged in minor criminal activity on a variety of scales and was well connected in the West End. What he liked best was little boys, particularly naughty, runaway Borstal boys. Litvinoff was physically quite ugly: thin lips, a huge nose and a prematurely bald head which he would attempt to disguise by smarming his hair from the back over his crown. But he could talk the birds out of the trees, money out of pockets, boys into bed, and gangsters out of killing him – except once, when the Krays sent a boy or two around to his Kensington High Street flat. They stripped him, tied him

59

to a chair, then razor-cut the corners of his mouth and hung him (still in the chair) out of the third-floor window. He hung there all night, dripping blood onto a Kensington pavement, as a lesson to any would-be big mouth.

The King's Road Sixties revolution was beginning. A whole new influx of pretty girls began to wander the King's Road looking for action, and we supplied it. Purple Hearts and Merrydown cider were the preferred drugs. If there was no party to go to at night, we would invade the West End jazz clubs: Sy Laurie's, Chris Barber's, or the All-Nighter in Wardour Street for a dose of Georgie Fame and the All Stars, or Graham Bond's R&B band, which was the best thing happening.

Peter Rachman and Raymond Nash, whom I knew well from my chemmie days, opened their nightclub in Wardour Street. Christine Keeler and Mandy Rice-Davies were there almost every night, and the casino in the back room was always alive with gambling action. The music was good too. Raymond Nash kept a permanent set of conga drums on the stage to indulge himself with, and he taught me to play.

It was around this time that I met Patrick Hutchinson, whose mother was the mayoress, or councillor, of a wealthy Norfolk market town, Wisbech. One afternoon in the Cozy, Cholmondeley, Johnny Somers, Patrick, a Spanish boy from Torremolinos named José and myself were having a one and ninepenny lunch when we decided to open our own coffee bar. Patrick said that his mother had a little premises in Wisbech that we could have for nothing. We were broke, but so hyped-up on speed that we hitchhiked to Norfolk. That summer we went barefoot, wore torn Levis and baggy sweaters. Our hair was long and we were none too clean; we thought we looked very interesting, as did the girls in the Wisbech High School.

The mayoress gave us a restaurant licence for the Aqua Brava coffee house and lent us some cash to decorate a little place in the market square. A Gaggia coffee machine was rented. The coffee house opened to a flurry of publicity, and was soon the talking point of Wisbech. Trouble started almost immediately. Tommy seduced a girl who could procure quantities of uppers and downers. This of course meant that the Palace Flophouse, as we had named the warehouse we were living in, was awash with little pills that some of us were swallowing all day long. Wisbech society was not ready for us.

The girls from the high school soon made the Aqua Brava their after-school hangout, which was great for us as we could take our pick. Young girls with crushes on beatniks in a small market town, however, was a recipe for disaster. Tommy's next conquest was the local hooker, who had a nice little house in the town where she serviced a few of the farmers and their sons and made a very good living. This was handy for Tommy, as betting shops had just been legalized and he missed the London dog-tracks.

The red lady's boyfriend and pimp was a rather wild didicoi called Frank. Inevitably, one day Frank came to the Aqua Brava looking for naughty Tommy. He had a sawn-off shotgun under his jacket and was not very friendly; he was also drunk. Tommy was washing up (something I took pleasure in making him do). He heard Frank's voice asking for him, and immediately slid down to the basement to hide. This was not a good move. Big Frank saw him, leapt the counter after him, and chaos ensued. Seconds later I heard the shotgun explode. Fearing the worst, I went down to the basement. There was no blood. Tommy had done it again, managing to chat his way out of trouble. He promised Frank that he would leave Susan alone unless he paid to see her like any other customer.

The shotgun blast had opened a long-locked door in our basement. We looked down the dark stone steps and descended to explore with matches. To our surprise we saw an abandoned entrance to the ancient stone-arched, oak-beamed, corn-exchange vaults, beautiful Georgian stone cellars reaching far under the old market square, unused for years. This became the Aqua Brava Jazz Club. Twice a week for the next couple of months we had a jazz band from the nearby American base playing to a packed house of GIs and farmers' sons. It finally closed when it was found to be a fire hazard.

I was doing too many Purple Hearts and dexedrine at this time. I needed rescuing, and Johnny Gilbert saved me. His father, Lewis, was about to make the film *HMS Defiant* with Alec Guinness, Dirk Bogarde and Anthony Quayle on location in Denja on the Costa Brava. We gave a great farewell party for the many friends we had made, the Aqua Brava served its last cappuccino, and we all took off.

Chapter Twelve

Terence Stamp had just made *Billy Budd* with Peter Ustinov in Denja. He had arrived back in London with his hair dyed blond looking like a Greek god. *Defiant* planned to use the same location and the same ships. David Bayliss offered to drive us there in his XK 120 Jaguar, and soon we were on the road again, to spend the summer in the charming little village of Denja.

Damn the Defiant, as it was eventually called, was a happy film. I was to be a pirate, Johnny an assistant director, and Lord Brabourne the producer. Lord Mountbatten came and spent a few days on the set, taking a particular interest in the script. The writer and director, Lewis Gilbert, put me in the thick of the battle scenes, and I relished every minute, swinging on ropes from galleon to galleon, brandishing cutlasses. Lewis decided that I should feature in a cutlass fight. My opponent was to be Mad Marcus. We survived rehearsals and the big day came. Hundreds of locals had been hired to boost the crews of the two ships that were to engage. Marcus and I stood by. Our cutlasses were made of a heavy, soft, blunt steel, but the blades had become viciously serrated with constant rehearsing. At last, our cue! I had to bounce off the rigging on the end of a rope and aim a blow at Marcus's thigh to start the fight off. He was meant to parry this, but he forgot. I caught him with a terrific slash. He completely lost it and suddenly I was fighting for my life. Lewis called cut. Marcus was not interested; our fight

63

continued across the deck around broken rigging to the cheers and gibes of our fellow extras. We eventually calmed down, exhausted, and covered in bruises. 'Terrific, boys, terrific,' said Lewis, knowing full well that the camera was nowhere near.

Eight weeks later, we were all back in the King's Road.

I wanted regular work in film but was in competition with hundreds of aspiring extras. After weeks of faithfully making calls to the Extras Union to no avail, I decided to take action. My mate Tommy Cholmondeley and I set off at four in the morning to hitchhike to Pinewood Studios wearing our fashionable cardboard boots made by Stan the Greek in Battersea. We had heard that the director Ruben Mamoulian was about to shoot *Cleopatra*. Every extra in the world knew about this. It was November 1960, snowing, and very cold. We watched more experienced extras as they were ushered in past the guard. A small crowd of hopefuls gathered as others began to join us. A man, who we learned was an assistant director, came out of the gate. He looked us over and said, 'You, you, you, and you, in.' This left Tommy and me on the pavement, blue with cold, the next morning and every morning for the next fourteen days. The weather got worse: ice, snow, wind and hail, until one morning, 'You two, in.'

The assistant first took us to the breakfast tent. Hot-air blowers and hundreds of Roman, Egyptian, and Macedonian soldiers drinking tea and scoffing bacon rolls. 'Have your breakfast and then get over to wardrobe, it's a marquee on block B.' At wardrobe, a woman said, 'Macedonian warrior,' and slid me a pile of gear consisting of a breastplate, thong skirt and sandals. 'Put that on and get over to make-up.'

The thong skirt came up under my armpits, the breastplate was made for Goliath, and the sandal thongs wrapped around what could be seen of my legs beneath the maxi-length skirt.

64

Thus attired, I struggled to make-up, goose pimples the size of dinosaur eggs covering my legs and arms.

'Stand on that stool.'

I did what I was told. From a bucket of brown paint the make-up assistant produced a huge brush and splashed me with Macedonian complexion.

When we met up in the warmth of the holding tent I discovered that Tommy had fared no better as a Roman centurion. There must have been three hundred of us in the huge marquee. You could tell the professional extras at a glance by their blankets. Somewhere in the studio Ruben Mamoulian was trying to make a film. We in the extras camp would never have known this. There was just a lot of card games and hanging about trying to keep warm. I collected seven pounds ten shillings for my day's work.

Several weeks later, I was already a professional and in a regular poker game with the stunt men and a few others. One was Freddie 'the Fox' AKA Troy Dante, a tall, good-looking, amiable cockney who knew the ropes. Freddie was full of information. 'Don't show your face when we get on the set. If they see your face on the rushes you get blown out.'

The day came of Cleopatra's entry into Rome, and there was a huge call for extras: Macedonians, Romans, Nubian slaves, and armies from the Roman colonies. The assistant directors toiled to set the scene, getting the lines of extras straight, removing wrist-watches, repairing make-up and costumes. Because the weather was so bad and the light so poor, every available light in the film industry had been commandeered to create a hot Roman day.

I met a huge fellow whom I knew from Soho, Peter Grant. A few years later he would be the most successful rock and roll manager in the world, steering Led Zeppelin up their 'stairway to heaven'. For now he was a Macedonian warrior like me, and I stood next to him in the front line.

Mamoulian was now on the set and riding one of the Mitchell cameras on its giant boom crane. He swooped up our noses, over our heads, and down the lines of warriors to the gates of Rome. The gates opened to reveal lines of Nubians towing Cleopatra on a sort of giant throne on wheels. Mamoulian zoomed towards me, riding his camera like a Harley Davidson. The jointed arm of the crane brought him to within a couple of feet of me. I stood there shivering. He pointed to me and beckoned. I looked at Peter Grant and Freddie the Fox who flanked me, as if to say, 'Bad luck, fellas, I'm on my way,' and stepped forward.

Ever so politely Ruben Mamoulian whispered in my ear, 'You are a bit small to be in the front, would you go around and get in the back row.' For the next few days I was known as back-row Mim. There was no mercy in the Extras Union.

Cleopatra was beset with problems. On 3 January 1961 Mamoulian resigned, and everything he shot was scrapped. The film did eventually get made, in Rome, starring Elizabeth Taylor and her new boyfriend Richard Burton, and directed by Joseph L. Mankiewicz. It was among the most expensive productions in history.

Chapter Thirteen

Dick Lester, rumour had it, was to make a film about a bunch of young kids trying to make it in the music business. I had just won the Twist contest that Associated Rediffusion had broadcast live on TV. The lovely Belinda was my dancing partner. In April 1962 I was back at Pinewood Studios, auditioning for Dick ('Running, Jumping, and Standing Still') Lester in his cubby-hole of an office. I twisted and jived and got the part of Helen Shapiro's dancing partner in *It's Trad Dad*. With Craig Douglas and one of my heroes, Gene Vincent, I jived my way through that, and through a film called *The Young Ones* with Cliff Richard's gang.

The Sixties was now officially on. Nicky and Kiki Byrne, Mary Quant and Alexander Plunket Green had opened their boutiques. The Road was one big party.

One afternoon I went to see a film called *Orfeuo Negro* which was showing at the Classic. I came out stunned. Directed by Marcel Camus, it had a wonderful, extraordinary soundtrack from the Rio Carnival. The drums never stop and the rhythms just sort of hang there throughout the film. It starred an amazing coffee-coloured Brazilian actress, Marpessa Dawn.

I went to the Gilded Cage for a coffee after the movie and there was Marpessa, even more beautiful in real life. I steamed in and told her how fantastic the film was, in genuine adulation, and, instead of telling me to get lost, she was very kind to me. In town to publicize the film, she had come down to the famous

King's Road to check it out. I was her guide, and saw her every day until she went off to the Cannes Film Festival.

Meanwhile a lunatic bearded actor/director, Peter Prowse, a six-foot-six South African with a bellowing Afrikaans accent, had written a play called *Boss Woman*. He knew I was a friend of Marpessa and asked if I would give her the script. 'There is a part for you in it,' he added.

I gave it to her on her return from Cannes. She liked it, and suddenly I was on the road. The play opened in Brighton. Marpessa got good reviews. My part turned out to be a walk-on, so I busied myself with learning stage management. At the Cambridge Arts Theatre it was hoped that the London managements would come and give the play a London theatre. By this time it was losing money hand over fist. Peter Prowse, who was also lead actor and director, had taken to the bottle and gone all moody because the reviews for his direction and performance were atrocious. The more pissed and unreliable Mr Prowse became, the more my workload increased.

My friend Lewis Gilbert came to the rescue. He had a word with the quintessential agent Stanley Dubens, son of Harry Dubens, the last of the old-time West End theatrical agents. Stanley ran his agency out of a shared office above the Soho Snooker Centre on the corner of Frith Street. I received a telegram from Lewis telling me that an important agent was coming to see the play, and I told the company we had a VIP coming to the evening performance, which bucked everybody up except for Peter, who was off the rails.

Down came the curtain. I told Mr Dubens that there was nothing wrong with the play that Rod Steiger in the Peter Prowse role couldn't cure, but when I finished my spiel he told me that the play stank. However, he said Lewis had spoken highly of me and that he was looking for an apprentice. He gave me a card and asked me to come and see him when I finished with the play.

68

Boss Woman folded on the Saturday night. Sunday found me at the Temperance Snooker Hall. The Dubens offer of an interview was floating around my brain. It was June 1962, I was twenty-one, and so far had avoided getting a proper job.

On Monday morning I put on the suit and took the number 14 bus to Soho. Finding the dingy entrance to the Stanley Dubens Theatrical Agency was easy: it was the same entrance as the Soho Snooker Centre, where I had spent many an all-night session. Stanley's offices were a couple of poky, partitioned rooms, the floor and desk stacked with scripts. Mr Dubens had an assistant, Jean Drysdale, and the office was also shared with a pair of literary agents, Richard Gregson and Gareth Wigan.

Jean gave me a script. 'Stanley would like you to read this. When you have, come back and he'll see you.'

I thanked her and went to the French Café in Wardour Street, the hangout of the Extras Union mafia. I walked in and ordered a coffee, nodding to some of the familiar faces, and settled down to read. It felt terrific sitting in the French with the script for a Hammer film. I read it, paid for my coffee, and strolled back to the Dubens office.

'What can you tell me about that?' said Stanley. I said that a friend of mine, Barbara Steele, would be right for the leading role. Barbara had been working with Fellini in *8½*, and had carved a name for herself in some horror films with Vincent Price.

'How well do you know her?' asked Stanley.

'I know her very well.'

'Good. Now I don't expect you to do much to start with. You can read the mail, read the scripts, go to the theatre and the drama schools, and listen to my phone calls. I'll give you a thousand pounds a year and out-of-pocket expenses. If you want the job you can start right away.'

'What actually is my job?'

69

'You are going to become a theatrical agent. I will teach you two golden rules. First, never give a bad actor a good part. Secondly, never give a good actor a bad part. In between that you have to earn a living. Now, here is our client list, and here are their credits.'

Stanley gave me a couple of sheets of paper. He had two stars: Kenneth More and Sylvia Syms. The other clients included John Horsley, Edward Underdown, Sam Kydd, and an actress called Dilys Ley.

'Do you want the job?'

'Yes,' I said, 'thank you.'

'Good,' he said. 'Start in the morning, nine o'clock.' Stanley picked up the phone and went to work. Jean showed me out of the office.

Lewis and Hilda Gilbert were very pleased for me, and promised to give me as much help in my new job as they could. Lewis was now very successful, and about to become more so.

Although I was now working for a living, nothing much had changed. I spent my evenings grooving on the King's Road or in Soho. Cindy Cassidy was back on the scene with a new boyfriend, a diminutive piano-player, Dudley Moore, the resident pianist at the Establishment Club in Greek Street. Dudley Moore and Peter Cook had joined forces with Millicent Martin and David Frost to create *Beyond the Fringe*, which became a major success. Just around the corner was the All-Nighter with its house band, Georgie Fame and Graham Bond, both of them virtuosos on the B3 Hammond organ. Sy Laurie's had folded; Chris Barber was resident at the 100 Club. The home of modern jazz was the basement club M in a hotel on the corner of Coventry Street.

Suddenly all the liggers were getting jobs, or going to work. Denny Cordell, John Fenton, Chris Stamp, Kit Lambert and Georgio Gomelsky were checking out the music business. I moved into the top floor of 23 Cadogan Gardens, a four-room flat I shared with Chris Stamp and a wild-boy actor named Clive Colin Bowler, who could have been a big star. Terry Stamp and his mate Michael Caine moved into Michael Wilding's *pied-à-terre* in a little street next to Buckingham Palace. Terry had raced ahead of Michael at this time. *Billy Budd* and *To Sir With Love*, in which he starred with Laurence Olivier and Sarah Miles, had booted him to stardom, but still the two East End mates were pretty inseparable. Michael's big break would be coming soon.

Chapter Fourteen

Our Cadogan Gardens flat was outrageous. Chris Stamp was better looking than his brother. Women flocked through the door. Naturally our new showbiz credentials greatly enhanced our success rate with the ladies. Vidal Sassoon's Curzon Street salon, and the photographic studios of David Bailey, Bob Freeman, Vic Singh and Terry Donovan were fantasy places: the most desirable girls in the world traipsed through these portals on a daily basis. Actresses, models, debutantes and shopgirls threw themselves into the action. Any pretty sighteseeing visitor to the King's Road was fair game. It was not unusual for five or six women a day to pass through the flat. The clap was prevalent too, but you didn't die from a one-night stand in those days; a couple of shots of antibiotic, no booze for a week, and you were back in business.

The English rock scene was on the verge of breaking. The Rolling Stones were making a name for themselves in Richmond. The All-Nighter had a regular flow of bands and musicians: the Yardbirds, the embryonic Led Zeppelin, Rod Stewart, Eric Clapton, John Mayall, Eric Burdon. Meanwhile, the Roaring Twenties, off Beak Street, would rock all night to the Skank and Ska saxophone of the incredible Roland Alphonso. Hanging out all night in Ladbroke Grove with Harry Baird, Speedy and Lucky was a very cool thing for a white boy to do. The backroom shebeens in and around All Saints Road would sell you a whiskey from the bottle or a joint, or a plate of curry goat, or rice 'n' peas. There were also a lot of drugs, but they were used to intensify the life-style – they had not yet become the life-style itself. Liquid methedrine was common as an all-night boost; cocaine, dexedrine, benzedrine, Purple Hearts and Black Bombers were all taken to keep us going through the long weekends. Grass, hash and amyl nitrate were for the bedroom.

Meanwhile Jean Drysdale, Stanley's assistant, had just signed a cute young girl with a turned-up nose fresh from Manchester via RADA. June Ritchie was about to get her big break. Stanley had organized a test for her with John Schlesinger, who was casting the film *A Kind of Loving*, and she had been shortlisted. Kenneth More and Sylvia Syms were household names and very much loved but the agency desperately needed a young star. June's screen test was great, so she got to play the part opposite Ian Hendry, and we all went to Iso's restaurant to celebrate. Jack Iso was the last of the Soho restaurateurs with flair. His establishment was a show business Mecca with customers' names on the backs of the chairs.

It was 1962, and a good time to be twenty-two and in show business. Although I was just a young agent, I was in the middle of the action. And I knew what I liked. My heroes were Kurosawa and Bunuel. Actors like Vladek Sheybal and the cast of the Polish film *Ashes and Diamonds* had made a great impression on me. Out of this school came Roman Polanski, who was preparing to come to England under the auspices of the producer Gene Kutowski. I worshipped Brando in *On the Waterfront*, Sam Spiegel, Fellini's *La Strada*, Lee Strasberg, James Dean, Marilyn Monroe, Rod Steiger, Karl Malden, Grisby, the French gangster movies and Jean Gabin. England did have Pinewood, and the Boulting Brothers at Shepperton made good films, but somehow there was nothing being made here that had the same romance for me as the American, French and Italian cinema.

73

Samantha Eggar, Sarah Miles, Susanna York, Julie Christie and Carol White were about to be the hot *ingénues* of British cinema, with Finney, Stamp, Courtenay, O'Toole, Bates and Tom Bell its young knights, with John Hurt and Michael Caine waiting in the wings.

I was befriended by young directors like Philip Savile and Waris Hussein, who were a great help. If I was lucky enough to be given the script of a project that had yet to be cast, I would rush back to the office, read it, cast it in my mind with actors from the Dubens client list, and then give it to Stanley or Jean, who would switch my casting ideas around, and then do the selling. As I gradually got my confidence, my own client list developed. Jean gave me the odd character actor to represent – Sam Kydd, John Horsley and Leslie Howard's brother Ronald.

I would attend all the drama school showcases, a harrowing experience. RADA was particularly difficult. It was like the Newmarket sales, a school full of thespian thoroughbreds. The little Vanborough Theatre was always full, and representatives from all of the theatrical agencies would be there.

On my first visit I walked into the theatre feeling quite important. I took a seat surrounded by my peers from the big agencies. We nodded politely to each other, the lights dimmed, and the curtain went up. The first snippet was a piece from *Hamlet*. Brian Marshal was brilliant. I couldn't wait to rush backstage and sign him. The next piece was a scene from *Borstal Boy* – John Forgeham, a big lump of a boy with a load of stage presence. I put a tick by his name. At the end I went backstage with the ticks on my programme: Albert Finney, Tom Courtenay, Brian Marshal, John Forgeham, Sarah Miles. The powerful agents had already sewn them up. Jean, who was with me, made a beeline for John Thaw. John Forgeham agreed to come to the office sometime for a chat. Brian Marshal also agreed to visit. Naturally, I didn't get Finney or Courtenay; I did end up signing Forgeham and Marshal.

I eventually got the hang of these meat markets. Flattery was the key, combined with big brags about what could be done for such talented young persons: 'Don't sign to a big agency, you'll get lost in the crowd.' I learned to be cynical, sympathetic, flattering and critical, charming and repugnant, persuasive and obstinate. Still naïve and fresh, I was now a hard-working young man . . . with a serious hedonistic streak.

As yet I had no major star to represent, so one day Stanley sent me down to Pinewood Studios for the day to see what I could find. At lunchtime in the studio bar I met a man who looked like he had been sentenced to the gallows. I introduced myself. His name was John Pennington. I told him I was an agent and we talked. He was in desperate need of a star for his film. I read his script in the sunshine over a pint of bitter. It was perfect for Kenneth More. Kenny was lovely but a bit stuck in the Fifties; he desperately needed a film. I went back into the bar and told Mr Pennington, 'Kenneth More should play this part.' I took the script back to the office, and gave it to Stanley. Stanley made the deal, and Kenny was working, starring in *The Comedy Man*. A few days after this I was made a director of the Stanley Dubens Theatrical Agency.

My reputation was slowly growing as my contacts increased. Stanley had taught me that contacts were everything, so I had the names of every casting director and their secretaries, every producer, their home and office addresses, their favourite restaurants. If word reached me that a producer had acquired the rights to a certain book, I would read it immediately, cast it in my head, and then work on trying to meet the guy. First I would call Mario or Franco at the Terrazza and ask who was having lunch today. If my quarry was not there I would call Bianchi's, Uncle Petty's place. I had to keep ahead of the game; as soon as a production was announced in the trades the company switchboard would be jammed with every agent in London trying to talk to the director, producer or casting director.

In those days the best casting directors were worth their weight in gold to producers, actors and agents alike. Maude Spector was the best. She could pop an actor into a three-line part and tell you it would make him or her a star – and she would be right. Sam Spiegel never made a movie without her.

My special mate was a brash New Yorker called Rose Tobias Shaw, head of casting for Lew and Lesley Grade at ATV. She would slip me episodes of *The Saint* to read or *The Baron* or *The Avengers*; useful bread and butter, particularly for actors who could be cast as young villains. All these programmes had male stars who needed new good-looking female leads each week. With Rose's help I was soon placing Gabriella Licudi, Edina Ronay, Imogen Hassall, Dana Gillespie, April Wilding, Anne Lawson, Danni Sheridan and Barbara Steele.

After office hours I was back on the King's Road. One night I popped in to see Diana Dors; she had phoned me sounding depressed. I arrived at her Chelsea house to find a small party in progress. I was not the only one she had called to discuss her depression. Dandy Kim and Andrew Ray were already there. Diana needed a man in her life, and over a bottle or two of champagne we all discussed her problem. I told her I had just the person for her. It so happened that my old mate Freddie the Fox had changed his name to Troy Dante and was now chasing a career as a pop star. He had come to see me that afternoon to ask me to manage Troy Dante and the Infernos. The newly invented Troy was good looking and had a lot of bottle. At Diana's suggestion I rang him.

'Troy! Tart yourself up and come to this address in Chelsea. I've a surprise for you. Just look good and come over.'

He showed up, looking like a Jess Conrad clone. I introduced him to Diana through the serving-hatch that went through the drawing-room wall to the kitchen. The chemistry was immediate. Troy took her hand through the hole in the wall, drew her to him, and kissed her. They were together on and off until Diana met Alan Lake.

One day I was having coffee with Samantha Eggar, a protégée of Dandy Kim's, in the poshest of the King's Road coffee bars, the Gilded Cage. She was learning her part for *The Collector*, a film she was to star in with her drama-school classmate Terence Stamp. A young man sat down at our table with some reels of film under his arms. He was a cool-looking New Yorker. I soon discovered his name was Seymour Cassel, an actor with the New York Actors' Workshop studying with John Cassavetes. He was carrying a print of a film, *Shadows*, he had produced with Cassavetes. Seymour had the task of bringing the film to London to look for publicity and a distribution deal. He was actually on his way to the Cannes Film Festival. We took the film down to the Classic on the King's Road, and arranged for a showing the next morning. *Shadows* was right up my street. Shot in black and white on the streets of New York, it starred Benito Carruthers and a gang of New York actors from the Workshop. Carruthers was the coolest thing I had seen since *Rififi*. A publicist I had invited, Joe Lustig, liked the film and promised to do some work.

Carruthers arrived in London and I organized a ticket for him to fly to Cannes on the promise that I could represent him in Europe. A week later *Shadows* won fantastic acclaim at the Festival. I had my first star, but Stanley was not overly impressed. *Shadows* was what Wardour Street termed an art film.

I was a huge fan of all the New York TV shows, particularly *Dragnet* and *Naked City*. The latter used a lot of method actors. In several episodes I had noticed a young actor called Dennis

Hopper, and I remembered his small part in *Rebel Without a Cause*. I thought he was brilliant. Rose had given me a script for an episode of *The Saint* which had a leading part for an American hoodlum. I mentioned Hopper to her. 'Go and get him for me,' she said.

I made a few phone calls and found myself talking to the man himself. He was delighted that an English agent should know his work, and had never been to England. I think I got him a thousand dollars, a round-trip ticket and a week at the Cumberland Hotel. I went to the airport to collect the *enfant terrible* of American television only to see a limping Hopper come through Customs, his left leg in plaster to the hip.

'Hey, man, sorry about the leg.'

I was freaked out. The shooting schedule of *The Saint* was very tight. Dennis was due on the set in the morning. Rose had waved all sorts of Equity problems aside to accommodate my casting idea. The part called for Dennis to ride a motor-bike like Lee Marvin in *The Wild Ones*, and my star was having trouble riding crutches.

'Why didn't you tell me?' I asked.

'You know, man, it just happened.'

I took him to Rose's Marble Arch office. 'Rose! Meet Dennis Hopper.'

I thought she should get the news the way I just had. She didn't bat an eyelid. She picked up the phone to the director.

'The Dennis Hopper character . . . he's such a maniac I think he should play the part with his leg in plaster. Yeah, thought you'd like it.'

She put the phone down. Then, as one New Yorker to another, she gave Dennis a blistering.

Chapter Fifteen

A cool, sophisticated American chap with loads of money had arrived in London. Victor Lowndes and his partner Hugh Hefner owned *Playboy* magazine and a chain of macho clubs in the States.

Victor's entry into London society was smooth. He gave great parties peppered with visiting Americans: Sammy Davis Jnr, Steve McQueen, Peter Lawford, James Coburn and, of course, lots of Bunnies. Us Chelsea lads loved him, and he loved us.

He found a building on Park Lane where he opened the first Playboy Club in Europe. There was great excitement as he started to recruit; he paid very well and with the help of imported Bunny Mothers had soon trained a litter of British Bunnies. My friends and I watched Victor carefully create the Park Lane Playboy Club, select the decorators, train the croupiers for the casino, build private VIP rooms on the top floor. It seemed that every interesting person in the world came to the opening night. The party made the Playboy VIP card the hottest ticket in town.

The euphoria of the Sixties was everywhere. Stanley had gotten carried away. He took me for a walk in Soho one day and showed me a new building, No. 58 Old Compton Street, Soho. 'I have rented the penthouse. Come and see your new office.'

Through the marble and terrazzo hall we went and up the

stainless-steel lift, emerging into an office high above Soho; it was perfect.

I had a crush at this time on a most beautiful, fawn-like creature, Patti Boyd. She lived with her parents in Barnes or Putney, and I used to see her on the number 14 bus as it passed my flat. Eventually, I got talking to her and we became friends.

One day at the office I had a call from Dick Lester. It was March 1964, and he was about to direct the Beatles in *A Hard Day's Night*. He knew I could always find pretty girls and he needed some. I called Patti and she came to my office. When she arrived I contacted the production manager, John Merriman, who gave me a call for five girls. Patti went along with Edina Ronay, Danni Sheridan and a couple of other young hopefuls. Patti called me that night to say that she'd had a great time and that George Harrison had asked her to dinner. I didn't see Patti again for fifteen years, by which time she had been Mrs Harrison and Mrs Clapton.

Chelsea was still the favoured playground. For a change of scene, Alvaro and Mimo had left the Trattoria Terrazza in Soho to open Alvaro's in the King's Road. Designed by Apicella, those twenty tables, whitewashed walls, linen tablecloths and trattoria food became the most exclusive in the world. I had a permanent table which I sort of leased out. Each night I would put together a bunch of interesting people, and rarely did I have to pick up the tab.

I was still living with Chris Stamp, and one day he came home with this weird guy full of adrenalin and Purple Hearts, Kit Lambert. I went off to see Chris and Kit's band, the High Numbers, at the Railway Hotel in Harrow. The place was a madhouse with hundreds of Vespa scooters outside. The band played a dynamite gig, and were soon re-christened The Who.

* * *

Ronan O'Rahilly had been very quiet since the Actors' Workshop in the old Chelsea studios had failed. His attempt at film production had not come to much – except for *Girl on a Motor Cycle* with Marianne Faithfull. But suddenly he was back, surfacing in true Sixties fashion, as out of nowhere sailed a ship called *Caroline* on which he'd installed a radio transmitter.

The music industry at this point was using the BBC and Radio Luxembourg to plug its records. On Easter Sunday 1964, Ronan and Radio Caroline put a stop to this monopoly. Chris Blackwell, Chris Stamp, Mickie Most, Shell Talmay, Andrew Oldham and Brian Epstein saturated the airwaves with the music of Spencer Davis, the Animals, the Rolling Stones, the Beatles and The Who. Ronan, sitting in his Curzon Street office with a bust of JFK on his desk, suddenly became the most powerful man in the music business. The records would be sent by launch out to the good ship *Caroline* with instructions to the DJs: 'saturation play'. *Caroline* quite simply made hit records out of great records; before this, saturation play was impossible. The BBC made rapid programming changes to compete, but Ronan stayed ahead of the game.

With every kid in England tuned to Radio Caroline, it didn't take a rocket scientist to work out that Ronan was the master of a potentially powerful and possibly dangerous voice. The Wilson government realized this, and spared nothing in an attempt to close him down, employing the best legal brains in the country. Until August 1967, when the Marine Offences bill took effect, Ronan kept the music coming and the ship afloat, weathering the storms of nature and politics to become the most notorious pirate of the Sixties.

I had a great address book by this time, and we could not fail to have fun. Michael Caine and my jiving partner Edina Ronay had become an item. Edina was pushing Johnny Gilbert, the associate producer, to get Michael the part of Alfie. Once again

Michael was up against Terry Stamp. Johnny went to see a rough cut of *The Ipcress File* and was immediately convinced that Caine was Alfie and campaigned accordingly. The clincher came when Terry opened in Bill Naughton's play on Broadway. It was a huge flop, Lewis Gilbert cast Michael in the film and the rest is history. *Alfie*'s success ensured that Michael would now go on to eclipse his old friend Terry Stamp.

One morning in 1965 I was reading my *Evening Standard* and checking the racing page when I noticed that a new cartoon had appeared underneath 'Garth'. Modesty Blaise was a female 007 with a cockney sidekick and an inscrutable butler. I went back to the office and rang the *Standard*; they put me through to Peter O'Donnell. He was an unassuming man who beavered away in his Fleet Street office, writing cartoon strips. I told him that I thought Modesty would make a great film heroine. An hour later I was at the Beaverbrook headquarters, sitting in Mr O'Donnell's cubby-hole of an office. As I thumbed through galley proofs of his *Modesty Blaise* novels, and piles of drawings of the cartoon, I became convinced that she would become the female James Bond. To my amazement the newspaper didn't own the film rights. I made a deal on the spot and took an option for three hundred pounds – a quarter of my yearly salary from the Dubens office. Stanley was always talking about options on this book or that, but I had never been involved in the packaging side of the business, and this was my chance. I went back to the office with my prize. I put the *Evening Standard* on Stanley's desk open at the racing page.

'Modesty Blaise,' I said.

'Which race is it in?' he asked.

'No, the cartoon. I've taken an option on the cartoon.'

Stanley read it and asked me how much I'd paid. I told him that I had offered O'Donnell three hundred pounds against a purchase price of three thousand pounds. 'I was hoping that you would give me an advance.'

Stanley looked at me. 'It is a good idea. We'll do it through the office.'

I agreed, and Stanley called Peter O'Donnell to check my story.

When I came into the office the next day there were some papers on my desk. I had been issued with one share in the company. I was over the moon. Jean, Stanley and I went to lunch at Iso's to celebrate. I was busy trying to cast *Modesty Blaise* from the actors on my client-list. Then I got a bit more realistic. Willie Garvin, Modesty's sidekick, was easy. Michael Caine was perfect and bankable. I had no doubt about Modesty herself. I had just the actress: Barbara Steele, although not a star yet, was fabulous — tall, thin, a mouthful of teeth, with legs that went on forever. And a favourite of Fellini's, which was good enough for me.

Stanley was rushing about Wardour Street looking for a deal. He either sold on the option, or bought out the rights and sold them on to Joe Janni's production company. I never really found out which, but I understood we had four per cent of the producer's gross.

Joe Janni was a big wheel and had several artists and directors under contract to him. Monica Vitti, an Italian yum-yum of the Gina Lollabrigida school, was his biggest name. He also had an option on the services of Joe Losey, a hot director at the time, so *Modesty Blaise* went into production. Terry Stamp was cast as Willie Garvin. Monica Vitti got the lead, and Dirk Bogarde was cast as Tarrant, the M figure.

I was easily squeezed out of the negotiations, which didn't upset me as I didn't know any better. What did upset me, however, was the film. As the production started to unfold my vision of a female James Bond blockbuster gradually faded. Monica Vitti padded around the film in bare feet. The heroine in my head wore stiletto heels. I was very disappointed when I saw a rough cut. The film did have charm but was far from exciting.

Stanley kept his spirits up in his usual effervescent way. After a couple of previews it was clear that we did not have a James Bond film on our hands, so he called me in and asked me if I knew anybody who might be interested in a percentage of the film.

I had been hanging out with this charming young knight of the realm, Sir William Pigott-Brown, owner of a huge estate in Berkshire, and heir to a banking fortune. William had a string of race horses and more cash than all the Las Vegas fruit-machines. I asked him if he would like to buy a piece of the *Modesty Blaise* film. The deal was simple. We owned points of the producer's gross which he could buy. If the film was a success he would make a fortune. I organized a screening and threw a little party with lots of pretty girls. Sir William enjoyed the party and the film.

We went out to dinner after the screening and Sir William was on the verge of agreeing to buy our percentage. It so happened that I had got to like this guy, he was great fun. So I told him what I really thought of the film. I said that, though quirky, it would be a commercial turkey and that if he wanted to invest in the movies I would find him something much healthier.

The next morning Stanley asked me how I had got on. I told him what had happened.

Chapter Sixteen

Within a week I rented a small room in Wardour House. I had use of the switchboard and my name was on the door: 'Emilio Scala Theatrical Agent'. I took Barbara Steele, Benito Carruthers, Edina Ronay, Jo Massot, Tom Bell's younger brother Keith, Mark Eden, and the foxy Danni Sheridan, who was living with me at the time. Danni and I had moved into a flat in Holland Park with Johnny Gilbert and Jean Nesbit. We made quite a foursome. Johnny was busy working on *Alfie*. He was responsible for instigating the inventive soundtrack, featuring master jazz saxophonist Sonny Rollins, which did much to help the film's street-cred.

Chris Blackwell arrived from Jamaica and opened a London office, keenly promoting what he was sure was the most exciting and untapped music in the world, reggae. He was just starting up Island Records when I met him, and was sharing a flat in Marble Arch with three fabulous Jamaican girls, Ester Anderson and Martine and Lorelie Beswick. Ester was a fireball, shrewd as a fox, with a temper like a volcano, and gorgeous. I fell for her and was soon two-timing Danni. Chris was pushing a young Millie Small and her record 'My Boy Lollipop'; Millie was looked after by the girls in the flat.

Another lodger was an amiable young Jamaican song-writer, Tony Washington. Tony helped me produce my first record, 'You Had Better Stop, Let Your Conscience Be Your Guide', with the Farinas (a band I'd found at Leicester Art College, who played the blues as good as any British band then). I signed the Farinas to Jack Bavistok, the head of the Fontana label at Philips, and we released the record in August 1964. When Johnny Gilbert finished working on *Alfie*, he took them on full time and turned them into a major international band, changing their name to Family.

We were suddenly all budding record producers. Denny Cordell, one of the gang from the Kenco, would soon be topping the charts with the Move and Procul Harum. Chris Blackwell had a huge hit with Millie and 'My Boy Lollipop', and was now working on the Spencer Davis Group with the brilliant young singer and organ-player Steve Winwood. Chris Stamp and Kit Lambert were pushing The Who. Music had become so important. If you could not play, or sing, you had to manage a band.

I sent Danni, Martine, and Ester off to audition for the James Bond film *From Russia With Love*. Martine was given the part of the wild gypsy girl who has the memorable hen-fight over Mr Bond in the gypsy encampment. Danni eventually went off to Switzerland to make *Casino Royale*, the next Bond film. Telly Savalas, playing Ernst Blofeld, fell for Danni on the set and started courting her. I didn't mind. Girl angst was the least of my problems. Around this time Jo Massot, the young Cuban who eventually directed *Wonderwall* for George Harrison, introduced me to Jacqueline Bisset, who had come up from Reading in search of fame and fortune. I was in love again, but she was snatched up by a movie biz heavy who shrewdly put her under contract. For the next few years he kept a tight rein on her. Only occasionally would she escape to come and play.

The Beatles were huge by now, with their seemingly all-powerful manager, Brian Epstein. So you can imagine my disbelief when the cheeky chappie Danny Buckley, the guy who invented the Gonks, showed me a piece of paper signed by David Jacobs and John Fenton giving him the rights to make the Beatle Gonks. This set off a chain of events. John Fenton, one of the King's Road gang, and Nicky Byrne saw Danny's enterprise as a sign. Fenton managed to persuade David Jacobs, Epstein's society lawyer, to sign away the Beatles merchandising rights to a gang of my King's Road mates. A hasty company was formed, Tramsact Ltd (incorporating smart backwards) in London, which issued a licence to dispose of Beatles merchandise to Seltaeb Inc. in New York. Now John Fenton, Nicky Byrne, Malcolm Evans, Simon Miller-Mundy, Mark Warman and the sublimely eccentric Lord Peregrine Eliot could market the Beatles, the biggest band in history.

I was too late to get involved in this money-spinning venture. I didn't see the lads for a bit, I just kept hearing rumours about how much money they were making. When I did get to New York on business in late 1963 I found them all ensconced in the Drake Hotel. The cash was rolling in, and they were lording it in New York on their Seltaeb proceeds. Epstein and Jacobs realized that they had made an atrocious deal for the Beatles and set about trying to sort out the merchandising mess for Nems, the Beatles' company. By this time fortunes were being paid to Seltaeb for rights to over four hundred and fifty items such as T-shirts, bubble gum and dolls. Nems were supposed to receive just ten per cent of Seltaeb's revenue – this was an incredibly bad deal, and Epstein knew it. As Jacobs put on pressure to close down the Seltaeb operation, eventually sending it pear-shaped, Nicky Byrne as the head of the company split to the Bahamas to await the outcome, and I guess get out of the way of some of the more disgruntled retailers, whose franchises and advances were now tied up in the litigation.

Tragically and coincidentally Brian Epstein died of an overdose as the Seltaeb story was being resolved. Shortly after this, David Jacobs was found hanged in his garage. These were strange times. Two incredibly successful men, at the height of their powers, dead within months of each other. I wondered, did they jump or were they pushed?

One of my clients was the inscrutable Michael Chow. Although moderately successful as an actor, he decided that what swinging London needed was a proper Chinese restaurant. He proceeded to open Mr Chow's. The Knightsbridge place was hip from day one. Chow had a rare feel for design. He rapidly acquired a collection of modern paintings. The food was outrageously expensive. The restaurant attracted artists and photographers like Peter Blake, Robert Brownjohn, David Bailey, Bob Freeman, Duffy, Vic Singh and Terence Donovan. They attracted the models, who in turn attracted the lads. The walls were soon covered with photographs of all the characters who came there to eat, as well as Blakes, Hockneys and Dines. Michael kept up his acting, featuring as a technician in *Dr No*, but he was to go on to become one of the great restaurateurs of London and Hollywood.

Meanwhile Chow's flatmate, Mike Sarne, had a number one record with 'Come Outside', and not to be outdone by Chow's success, hustled a deal to direct the film *Myra Breckinridge*, unfortunately a flop. However, he did end up marrying one of the girls from our office, the talented Tanya Gordon, who would eventually create the fashion empire Ghost.

It was cool to be busy – everyone was working. A generation of young creative people had exploded onto the scene. The music and film industries had been dominated by elderly bosses, but now the old boys were giving the young ones their heads. This didn't mean that we knew what we were doing. Very few of the new entrepreneurs kept the fortunes they'd instigated. Frankly I didn't care about the mistakes I made. I enjoyed making money, but the other people around me were better at it. So I blundered on, enjoying life and the roller-coaster of the Sixties.

Mim serving at his station in the ice creamery, 1957. The haircut is getting there.
(*Bernard Scala*)

Mim's other life. Seven debs' delights tank up at the New Inn, Hatherope,
Gloucestershire, after a ball for Miss Serina Gillilan at Hatherope Castle, 1958.
Left to right, Andrew Simpson with, *centre*, David Bellew, *far right*, Robin Sutherland,
and Mim on scooter. (*Alan Travers-Brown*)

Michael Caborn-Waterfield, a.k.a. Dandy Kim, with his Great Dane, Daiquiri and Samantha Eggar, before her Oscar nomination for *The Collector*, 1965.

Above right, Dandy Kim with Billy Hill – self-styled king of London's underworld before the Kray Brothers took over – outside the Rock Hotel, Gibraltar, 1959.

Opposite, Mim, apprentice agent in the new Stanley Dubens office, 52 Old Compton Street, 1963. (*Vic Singh*)

Opposite below, Michael Caine, *left*, addresses director Lewis Gilbert, *seated with cigar*, while Johnny Gilbert, *right*, chats up Millicent Martin, on the set of *Alfie*, 1966. *Inset*, Mim, also on the set of *Alfie* in the doorway of the 'Emilio Scala Maternity Hospital' – Lewis Gilbert's little joke. (*Vic Singh*)

The Mardi Gras girls at the Prospect of Whitby in London's East End, 1958. Johnny Gilbert, *left*, Wilhelmina Posy Morell with whippet, and Mim.

Right Mim as stage manager at Golder's Green Empire Theatre, getting in the set for *Boss Woman*, 1959. (*Hamish Grimes*)

Mim and Marlene Schroeder in New York, December 1967, before Salvador Dali's dinnner at the St Regis Hotel.

Above Mim and Harry Baird at the Playboy Club in London's Park Lane, 1967.

Right Mim with William Pigott-Brown and friend in Palma, Mallorca, 1967.

After work, we would be out playing again. The evenings progressed from drinks to dinner to the nightclubs. Eventually the entire gang would head for Jermyn Street. Johnny Gold had opened a club called Tramp, the last port of call for the serious revellers. Sir William and I had a semi-permanent table reserved at the back of the restaurant. We watched celebrities from Paris, New York and Hollywood flock in. They were all there, rocking at three in the morning, any morning: the Stones, the Beatles, Caine, Stamp, Victor Lowndes, Jackie Collins, Richard Harris, Sammy Davis Jnr, Rod Stewart, The Who.

The premises that Tramp occupied had been decorated for a mistress of King George. The room used for the dining-room had signs of the zodiac on the ceiling. At the back of this room was an alcove which housed the biggest table in the place: ours. There were two secret cupboards built into the oak panelling at the back of this table; one was used for storing china; the other we surreptitiously used for screwing during long evenings of combined business and pleasure.

One night I was at a table with Johnny Gaydon, David Enthoven and Willie Robertson, all of us high as kites. Johnny and David were at the height of their powers. Their company E.G. Records was to sign T. Rex, Brian Ferry, King Crimson, and Emerson, Lake and Palmer. Willie Robertson was an amiable, hard-working insurance broker at Lloyds, who could be quite outrageous, and was trying to break new ground by insuring the high-risk rock business.

Keith Moon was at the next table, crazy, and uninsurable. Willie, whose straight public-school exterior concealed a lunatic jester, had other ideas. He staggered to his feet, and offered a toast to the forthcoming Who tour, adding calmly, 'A tour that I would dearly love to insure.' Keith Moon apparently liked his approach and said, 'Take off your shoes and socks and step in every dinner on the tables.'

Willie whipped off his shoes and socks and immediately

began jumping from table to table, squishing mashed potatoes between his toes, to cheers of encouragement from the diners. Keith picked up the tab, and Willie got the insurance. He is still the most successful insurer of rock concerts in the world.

One day I received a strange phone call from a man called Michael Wilson. To this day I do not know how it came about. He told me that he had heard I was a very good agent. I listened. He asked if I was free to visit him at the London Hilton that evening. I said I was. I rushed home for a clean shirt and pressed my suit. Ready for business, I walked into the reception of the Park Lane Hilton. The lift opened into the penthouse suite when it stopped at the top floor. There was a bearded figure with a ponytail and pirate thigh-high boots, standing in the semi-darkness. Candles on the floor illuminated what looked like congealed lumps of gold or silver. They were in fact coral-encrusted pieces of eight and other lumps of treasure gleaned from some ancient wreck which Michael claimed he and a man named Arthur C. Clarke had discovered. With an arm around my shoulder, he walked me through to the main reception room and introduced me to three men I'd never heard of: Ray Bradbury, Satyajit Ray and Arthur C. Clarke. They sat around a coffee-table covered by telegrams, papers, and film scripts. Much to my surprise, Michael introduced me as his agent.

The script on the table was entitled 'The Alien', the telegrams were from agents representing Marlon Brando and Peter Sellers among others. The film would be directed by Satyajit Ray, from a screenplay by Ray Bradbury, based on a story by Arthur C. Clarke and Michael Wilson. Michael explained that a number of stars wanted to play the part of the alien, but they needed to raise pre-production money to get the project going, which was to be my job it seemed.

I walked back to Soho with the script under my arm, wondering desperately what to do next. The first thing was

90

to read the script. This I did. Thirteen of the world's most powerful men have received an invitation they cannot refuse to meet on a lakeside in India. During the meeting a sphere rises from the lake and out of it steps the alien, bearing instructions to the all-powerful ones on how to save the earth. This was not your usual Hammer filmscript, but with Brando or Sellers playing the alien I could see the commercial possibilities. I worked very hard on this project and somehow the pre-production money was raised. Wilson and Co. went off to L.A., checking into the Chateau Marmont Hotel, where they stayed for a month or so. I received the news later that the project was to be cancelled. I called Michael, who was quite philosophical.

'It's too far out, man. They're not ready for this kind of movie. But thanks for your help. If you ever want a beautiful holiday, come and visit us in Ceylon.'

We moved to opulent premises in Davis Street next to Claridges. Sir William and I were partners in the new agency; he would finance it, while I would run it. By the time the decorators had finished, Scala Brown Associates had a most prestigious modern office.

In the autumn of 1965 Chris Blackwell came over to Scala Brown Associates to play us his latest record by Steve Winwood and the Spencer Davis Group, 'Keep on Running', written by Jackie Edwards. It was contagious. We played it ten times straight off. Chris was looking for cash to promote the record and his fledgling record label properly. He had taken an office in Oxford Street and had signed Spencer Davis to Philips on the Fontana label. William liked Chris and agreed with me that 'Keep on Running' was going to be a smash. He loaned Chris the money, on the condition that if it was not repaid by a specific date William would gain a hefty percentage of Island Records. Chris took the loan, knowing this wouldn't happen, and went to work. The record went all the way and Winwood and Island Records never looked back. Chris did part with one share in the company, which he gave to Ester Anderson for services to the fledgling company. She kept that share until well into the Eighties, by which time it was worth a fortune.

Scala Brown Associates had gone psychedelic. William and I had changed tailors. He naturally had a vast wardrobe of handmade shirts, jackets and suits. He now added a row of kaftans, a bead rack, and a frilly shirt department. He was always immaculately dressed, even as a psychedelic hippie. The Mr Vincent suits gradually made way for Thea Porter, Mr Fish and John Crittle. We opened our own tailor shop, Sharks, with Leigh Davis and John Scott, who would later make millions with his FU jeans. The shops were in South Molton Street. Brown's was upstairs and run for us by Peter Hamilton Davis and his wife, Polly Barker, who supplied us with accessories.

We also bought the floundering *London Life* magazine, changing its name to *Look of London*. I was appointed editor, but rapidly relinquished the position, assigning it to our advertising manager Ross Benson. We published fortnightly, but even Benson's sterling efforts couldn't bring in enough income; the circulation of twenty thousand was too low, and we were up against *Queen* and *Tatler*. Still, it was a useful vehicle for starting trends and promoting our interests.

William acquired a major share in the new, trendy Sybilla's nightclub. The opening party, at which the Beatles turned up with Brian Jones, was quite fantastic. We were flying so high. I was taking acid almost every day to keep up all night, and I started to lose it. I was not the only one over-indulging. The trick was to know it. Powerful LSD was coming in from America, 1000-microgram windowpanes, little gelatine squares, Purple Haze, White Lightning – all extremely trippy.

Vic Singh, who had shot the credits for *Alfie*, was one of the most remarkable photographers of the early Sixties, the first Asian to break into the mainstream fashion world. His experimental pop videos for Island Records were to set trends. Vic and a young film editor with a promising reputation called Keith Green persuaded the Beatles to let them make a documentary based on the song 'A Day in the Life', commemorating the untimely death of the Byronic ('He didn't notice that the lights had changed') Tara Browne, a friend of mine as well as theirs. But Vic and Keith never came back from this project, or were so radically changed their careers just seemed to stop. They both suddenly withdrew from the scene, renouncing the material business world. These were heavy psychedelic times, and there were perceived casualties. Vic withdrew to dedicate the next decade to the study of time and light, in search of the perfect photograph, destroying much of his fabulous archive of images which had captured the major happenings of Sixties fashion and the evolution of the King's Road.

At Apple, George Harrison had a film project of his own called *Wonderwall*, and hired Jo Massot, the Cuban director I represented, and another Cuban exile, the writer Giamo Enfonte. Iain Quarrier and Sean Lynch went off to work on it.

I heard on the grapevine that fellow agent Barry Krost was struggling, and I persuaded William to acquire his agency, which had a good client-list of actors and directors. At the same time literary agent Bea Narazano joined the agency with her clients.

We changed the name of the company as a concession to our new partners – Scala, Brown and Krost was too much of a mouthful. We became the Confederates Agency, and Barry brought with him the young director Peter Collinson, who immediately started to package *The Italian Job* with Michael Caine.

93

The office now had a load of potential. Adie Hunter, Tanya Gordon and Amanda Sturge looked after Barry, Gaston de Chalus and myself. William was chairman, and his secretary Vanessa Grant was chief hen. The company Rolls was lined in Thea Porter paisley silk. I had a sweet little penthouse flat overlooking Hyde Park. The weekend parties at Aston Upthorpe were now notorious. The Playboy Club was in full swing. Alvaro had opened the Arethusa. We were surfing on the crest of a Sixties wave. Life was one twenty-four-hour groove. Something had to give.

Harry Baird, the Gentle Giant, walked into the office one day with a huge handsome black man, Jim Brown, the running back for the Cleveland Browns. They wanted to show me a film. There was a cinema in the Connaught Hotel which Sammy Davis Jnr had booked for his personal use. I rang him and borrowed it. Harry, Jim, Sammy, Peter Lawford, Dick Donner, the dope guru Sid Keiser and I watched the film, a collection of Jim's best touchdowns. It was easy to see why he was the highest-paid football player in the US. We sat there applauding each touchdown. Jim was devastatingly handsome, immensely strong, and he wanted to be an actor.

Robert Aldrich, director of *The Dirty Dozen*, offered him the part of Robert Jefferson. I read the script and it was perfect. The character had to run five hundred yards dropping grenades down the smokestacks of German bunkers. Benito Carruthers joined the cast, along with Lee Marvin, Charles Bronson and Al Mancini.

So Jim became a client. He hung out at the Playboy Club and became Danni Sheridan's boyfriend for a while until she moved to Hollywood to live with Telly Savalas. One time we lent him some badly needed cash, and to thank me for the loan he took me back to the Playboy. Harry was there with Victor Lowndes, and Muhammad Ali, and the great boxer's manager,

94

Elijah Muhammad, plus entourage. (Ali had changed his name from Cassius Clay after beating Sonny Liston in February 1964.) Victor was hosting the boxer's camp in the VIP suites. Victor and I were the only white men present. Jim had a discussion with the Ali camp and I was allowed to stay.

On 21 May 1966 at the Arsenal Stadium we had ringside seats to watch Muhammad Ali and Henry Cooper battle it out in their second confrontation.

I had witnessed their first encounter at Wembley Stadium in June 1963. Henry caught Cassius Clay with a right hand which poleaxed him, but he was saved by the bell. Angelo Dundee, one of boxing's shrewdest fight managers, had tried to revive the champ and just as it seemed all over, he'd raised Clay's glove. It was split. The delay let Clay recover and fight back to cut Henry's vulnerable eye during the fifth round.

This time, however, Henry Cooper was well beaten and had a split eye in the sixth round. I came away with a speck of his gallant blood on my Mr Fish shirt.

I was at the BBC one day for a meeting with the director Philip Savile. Passing a door in the great circular building, I heard the strangest music coming from within. I knocked and entered. It was the headquarters of the BBC Radiophonic Workshop. Inside were musical boffins headed by a man called David Vorhouse. As well as the *Dr Who* soundtrack and effects, the musicians in this workshop had made hours of electronic music, using a minimum of conventional instruments. I took a tape of their creations to Chris Blackwell, who signed the band. *White Noise*, released on Island later in 1967, was the first purely electronic album. It was to influence a generation of music-makers.

One evening, 25 November 1966, I heard that Chas Chandler (the bassist with the Animals), Mike Jeffreys, Chris Stamp, Kit Lambert and Danny Secunda were showcasing a US artist at the Bag of Nails in Mayfair. We headed over.

95

The street outside was packed. Every musician in town was at the door. Graham Bond, some of Georgie Fame's band, Jimmy Page and the Yardbirds, Eric Clapton – the list was endless. We had no trouble getting in, and were soon drugged up and drinking at the bar. The Jimi Hendrix Experience walked on stage.

In one set Jimi put himself beyond the English wizards of rock. Hendrix was from outer space. He could do anything the blues guys could do, but he had taken the Fender into the stratosphere. Jimi played that night what everybody else was thinking. Jimi played that night what everybody wanted to play. Jimi looked that night the way everybody wanted to look. His performance was to have a huge effect on the whole London scene. Chas Chandler was immediately elevated from an average bassist to a rock guru. Mike Jeffreys, Kit Lambert and Chris Stamp signed Jimi to their Yamita company.

Psychedelic rock and roll had arrived. Within weeks the style of my generation radically changed. Silk, velvet, beads, bandannas, uncompromising footwear, acid, hash, grass, speed, incense, fame, creativity in art, photography and music swelled out into the suburbs. New bands appeared as if overnight; old ones started writing with a new intensity. The King's Road was full of new shops catering to this revolution.

The clubs in the West End also changed. An interested party wandering around Soho at night would hear the Yardbirds, the Animals, Alexis Korner, Hendrix, all playing in accessible places. A kid could walk off the street and into incredible music. The late-night scene itself was more difficult to infiltrate. The hardcore players of Sixties London had their exclusive hang-outs: Sybilla's, the Revolution, the Scene, the Baghdad House.

A charming, conscientious young agent named Morgan Rees-Williams came to work with us. Elisabeth Harris, the wife of Richard Harris, was his sister. Richard became a client of the agency. His performance in *Mutiny on the Bounty* and in *This Sporting Life*, opposite Billie Whitelaw, together with his portrayal of Oliver Cromwell, had catapulted him to a position of maximum potential, up there with Finney, McQueen and Brando. *Camelot* had him singing in a suit of silver armour, riding a horse that was prettier than he was. Being outspoken, single minded, obstreperous, romantic, Irish, handsome and talented was too much of a package for one young man to handle, and it was at this time that Richard joined the ranks of the charming superstar hell raisers. Richard had been very well advised and looked after during the *Camelot* deal, and the contract was to make him a very wealthy man. He took time out to involve himself in an interesting production of Gogol's *Diary of a Mad Man* at the Royal Court, an incredible *tour de force*.

But Richard was far from finished. While in Hollywood, he had made friends with the talented lyric and song writer Jimmy Webb, and together they had cut some demo tracks. I played these to Sammy Davis Jnr, who was signed to Columbia records at the time. Sammy sent a Columbia executive to see me. He offered Richard a recording contract, but I could not persuade Richard to sign it and the deal fell away. Jimmy Webb persevered and eventually they collaborated on a very successful album, *MacArthur Park*. Richard's career revived when he made the film *A Man Called Horse* for Eliot Silverstein.

During the Scala Brown period Richard was having real trouble with his marriage. He really loved Liz, she was everything he was not: the daughter of Lord Ogmore, she was an Irish lady, beautiful, mannered, and educated; Richard was hard on the outside and soft in the centre. I have no doubt that she loved him, and he her. Constant rows strained the relationship, until it became impossible. Richard would pull himself together, apologize as only a charming Irishman can, re-establish for a week or two, and then crash. Sir William didn't help matters, he developed the hots for Elisabeth and was soon utilizing his considerable charm and power in an attempt to seduce her. It would take years for their relationship to revive and mellow.

Roman Polanski was getting married to the beautiful Sharon Tate, and Victor Lowndes offered to host his stag-night at the Playboy Club and later at Victor's town house. The guests included Richard, Terence Stamp, Michael Caine, Iain Quarrier, Steve McQueen, Warren Beatty, Harry Baird, Gene Katowski – Polanski's producer – and myself.

The party started off in the normal fashion, drinks, a joint or two, small talk. We all knew each other pretty well. We were being waited on by the pick of the Playboy Bunnies and a dozen other gorgeous girls. The higher and drunker I got, the more outrageous the party became. I was sharing the sauna with Michael Caine, Gene Katowski, and several of the girls, when the door opened and Richard staggered in. We all carried on with what we were doing. 'Come on you filthy bastards, come with me. I know where the real action is' – whereupon he staggered out of the heat. Michael, Gene and I were not about to leave. As morning came and Roman had to prepare for his wedding, we discovered what had happened to Richard. He had burgled Sharon's hen party, the only male present at that gathering of twenty of the most beautiful girls in London. He was unable to remember a thing.

The company Richard kept on his benders differed tremendously, depending on where he got drunk. If he was working or needed for a meeting, I would spend a few days with him so as to know at short notice where he was. Liz Harris was beautiful. Sir William developed a huge crush on her and took on the job of consoling her during Richard's disappearances. When he got the fever for a lady he would, and could, turn on considerable charm, utilizing his entire arsenal. His most powerful pulling asset was his estate, Orchard House at Aston Upthorpe, now part of the Maktoum racing empire, then one of the most charming estates on the Berkshire Downs: eighteen hundred acres of prime land, gallops for the horses, neat rows of stables, all painted the blue of William's racing colours. Every cottage on the estate was immaculate, with blue windows, doors and drainpipes.

Several of the cottages were rented to friends. The artist Michael Tain had one, as did Dave Dick. Steve Winwood and Jim Capaldi moved Traffic (Winwood's new band) into one of them. The Traffic cottage was presided over by Steve's girlfriend, the sexy and interesting Trinidadian Penny Farrar, my old jiving partner from the Mardi Gras. Friday nights would see a procession of cars whisking us all along the M4 for weekend house-parties. Promiscuity was king, and everybody got laid, stoned and drunk in the highest possible fashion.

William, fortunately, had the services of a husband-and-wife housekeeping team. George, an ex-policeman, was a miracle man who maintained the house and gardens fastidiously, with not a blade of grass out of place. The vast lawns that swept down to the floodlit pool were kept like a putting-green. The shrubs and flower-beds looked like the Chelsea Flower Show. An average weekend house-party usually consisted of about twenty people – the women beautiful, the men interesting, most of us raving.

George the butler took it all in his stride. Before breakfast he could be seen in full black-tie, trundling a smart wheelbarrow through the garden, nonchalantly ignoring Brian Jones, Jimi Hendrix, myself and female friends tripping in the pool at dawn, gliding past, picking up crystal glasses and empty bottles, knickers, bras, used amyls, and any other detritus from the night before.

William had several good stallions standing at stud in the stables. The National Hunt jockey and Grand National winner Dave Dick was his stud manager, a ladies' man of the old school. This new wave of womanizing and decadence was a bit much for him. He'd been William's mentor and had taught him to ride properly, coaching him through his Cheltenham National Hunt Chase victory on Superfine in 1961. As a reward he now ran the stud, but felt deeply out of place at breakfast giving William his report on weekly progress, with naked Miss Worlds and a bunch of hippies tripping out from the night before.

William had a wicked streak. I arrived at Aston Upthorpe early one weekend. We had some CBS executives coming for dinner. George took my bags up to my room and I noticed a new painting by Michael Tain on the wall. It showed a naked woman in thigh-length boots carrying a riding whip. The face was that of Liz Harris, and it was a good likeness.

George put down my bag and removed the picture. Richard Harris was on the guest list. The picture was to hang in Richard's bedroom. It was going to be one of those weekends.

Chapter Seventeen

Marlene Schroeder swaggered into the Revolution wearing nothing but a mink coat. I couldn't take my eyes off her. She stood next to me at the bar smelling irresistibly of expensive perfume and animal fur.

'Are you just going to stare at me or buy me a drink?'

It was late and a jam was in progress with Brian Jones, Hendrix and Keith Moon. I asked the club manager for a bottle of champagne. Marlene and I dug the jam and I invited her to join us after the gig. I was about to drive down to Aston Upthorpe for the weekend. I had an old Willis jeep outside and was planning to take Brian and Jimi with me. Marlene appeared to be a bit distressed but jumped at the invitation. She wanted to pick up a few things first, so we piled into the jeep and drove around the corner to Claridges, followed by Brian, Jimi, and their girls in Brian's chauffeur-driven Bentley. A porter emerged with a pile of Louis Vuitton and loaded up the jeep. It turned out that Marlene was the guest of one Huntington Hartford, who had ensconced her in a suite at the famous hotel. But she was having no fun.

We became good friends after that weekend, and several weeks later I received a ticket in the post with a note from Marlene inviting me to spend Christmas and New Year 1968 with her in New York. I decided to accept. Michael White asked me if I would go and look at a show called *Hair* for him, playing at the Panther Theater off Broadway.

'If you like the musical, bid up to ten grand for the rights.'

Marlene came to meet me at the airport in a stretch limo and whisked me away to a massive penthouse on 67th Street. There were incredible views of the city even from the jacuzzi. The apartment was obviously not hers but I made myself at home and asked no questions. We had loads of fun running around town that Christmas. When I told her about going to see *Hair*, she was enthusiastic and asked could she bring along a few friends. We met for a pre-theatre drink at Elaine's. Her friends turned out to be Salvador Dali and Abdul Matti Klarvine, the artist who painted the psychedelic, erotic Santana album covers.

Dali hated *Hair*, and his opinion was contagious. I agreed – in hindsight a big mistake. But meanwhile, Dali invited us to join him for New Year's Eve dinner in his suite at the St Regis Hotel.

Marlene and I got dressed up in our finest kaftanery, I had a few big lines and half a tab, and headed for the St Regis. After a trippy subway ride, we arrived at the hotel reception and were shown up to Dali's suite, which consisted of the whole floor of one wing. The rooms at the St Regis were separated by movable partitions. As we entered the suite we could see that all the partitions had been wound back to make one very impressive long room. The space resembled a medieval long gallery, empty save for three small wrought-iron garden tables at one end, each of which had two matching chairs. At the far end of the room was an ornate fireplace with logs burning. A huge choirboy's cassock with a frill collar was spread out carefully on the floor. It was perhaps twenty feet long. The only other furnishings were candelabra scattered about the place, the only source of light. Marlene and I were alone there at first, wondering what was going on. Abdul Matti and his English partner Katrine Milinaire, the daughter of the Duchess of Bedford, were next to arrive. We chatted and milled about, bemused in the huge space waiting for our host.

Dali and his wife Gala arrived eventually. He said nothing and sat himself down at the middle table. Waiters appeared with a *maitre d'*, who showed us to our seats. The little tables were placed far enough apart that conversation between the guests and the host was impossible. A sumptuous St Regis dinner was wheeled in on trolleys. We ate in silence. In the candlelight it was near impossible to make eye contact with the other diners.

Marlene and I were cracking up, enjoying being in the centre of a Salvador Dali Happening. After several courses and delicious wine, waiters appeared to clear away and replenish until all was quiet and we sat at our tables sipping brandy. A door opened at the far end of the room and we heard the sweetest singing. The source of the voices soon became evident as a line of young boys in full choir regalia trooped into the room accompanied by a black-gowned priest. The children formed a circle around the huge cassock on the floor. The tiniest one of the choristers climbed into the neck of the giant garment and began to sing: a tiny head in a huge body, singing like an angel in Portuguese.

Once the singing stopped, the doors on the left-hand side of the long room opened and the New York paparazzi charged in, flashing cameras as Dali stood up and posed in his cape and walking-stick. He came over to our table, shook hands with us and, followed by Gala, left. The paparazzi followed the maestro in pursuit of one last shot.

Chapter Eighteen

By 1968 the agency had some big stars – Christopher Plummer, Richard Harris, Jim Brown, and a stable of up-and-coming young actresses and actors like my good friend Harry Baird. I had put Harry in a film that was directed by Melvin Van Peebles in Paris. Barbara Steele was also working in Paris, so I flew over to see them and check out their progress.

We had a great weekend. French cinema was at the height of its influence. Rock and roll had not crossed the channel and there was a marked difference on the streets between London and Paris. There was no psychedelia on the boulevard St-Michel.

I took Barbara and Harry to Castells, the 'in' nightclub, and found myself in a deep conversation with one of my heroes, Jean-Luc Godard, who had made *Alphaville* with Julie Christie, and *Pierrot le Fou* with Jean-Paul Belmondo, both of which I loved. As we talked over the music of Traffic and Otis Redding I discovered that Godard had never worked in England. I told him of the revolution we were experiencing in London, and about the Beatles and the Rolling Stones. I was amazed that such an influential film director didn't seem to be aware of what was happening, and promised to provide him with some music.

On my return to London, I sent him a few records and then forgot about it until I got a call from a woman named Elaine Collard, who told me that she was Godard's producer, and asked if it would be possible for him to make a film with the Beatles or the Stones.

I asked her to have Godard send me a script of his idea and said I'd get it to Mick Jagger and/or John Lennon. I received a letter from Godard a week later: 'My film will have a beginning, a middle and an end, but not necessarily in that order.' I loved it. He was getting psychedelic.

I rang Sandy Leiberson, a fellow agent at CMA, who represented the Stones for films. I also called John Lennon at Apple asking if the Beatles would consider making a film with the director of *Alphaville*. I sent both bands a copy of the Godard letter. Both said 'yes' in principle the following day. In the meantime Michael Pearson had set up a film company called Cupid with another of my clients, Iain Quarrier. Michael agreed to finance the film without even seeing a script, just the one-page letter from Godard. Buzzing, I returned to my office. In a few days I had put together the basic package of what I believed to be a major movie, with the choice of the Stones or the Beatles. I called Godard.

'I have the finance. When do you want to start, and who do you want to use?'

He asked me what I thought best – which I found odd, so I told him that, personally, I believed the Stones should be his choice: Dick Lester had already cinematically exposed the Beatles but the Rolling Stones as a band were still film virgins. He said that he would listen to the music and think about it, so I sent him a demotape of 'Sympathy for the Devil' that I had hustled from Jimmy Miller. At the same time I received a series of calls from Apple and John Lennon demanding an answer.

'Who's doing this fucking Godard film, the Stones or us?'

The word was out. Michael and Iain had a meeting with Paul McCartney and George Harrison, at which it became apparent tht the Beatles were far too busy anyhow. I had a call from Godard two days later.

'The film will star my wife, Anne Wiazemsky, Frankie Dymon Jnr. the black activist and the Rolling Stones.'

Iain Quarrier and I went to Sandy Leiberson's office and hammered out a deal. This done, I called Lennon at Apple and told him of Godard's decision; he took it on the chin. One more project that the Beatles did not have to worry about. The Stones were working with Jimmy Miller at this time preparing to record 'Sympathy for the Devil' for the album *Beggar's Banquet*. Sandy agreed to let us have the Stones for a total of six days for what was then a lot of money, peanuts now.

The small offices of Cupid Films in New Bond Street became a hive of activity as the Godard crew was assembled. Michael Pearson and Iain Quarrier were to be executive producers. I slipped into the background.

The chaotic method of film-making that Godard applied to this particular production soon became apparent. The first problem arose when he declared that he would shoot the film in eight millimetre, a nice arty idea which would render the film almost unreleasable. Cupid had to persuade the master director to at least shoot it in sixteen. Secondly, there was tension between Godard and his wife, who was playing the female lead. Thirdly, the one-page script left a lot to be desired. The production started each day with the playing out of a new incoherent mystery. This, plus the fact that the Stones were busy recording, made scheduling a nightmare.

The film rolled along until one morning I went to the Hilton where the Godard camp were installed. It was the film's first day in Olympic Studios. I went to reception and asked for Godard.

'I am sorry, sir. He and his party have checked out. They left for Paris this morning.'

It was now 8 a.m. I was stunned. I was supposed to take the crew to Olympic to introduce them to Jimmy Miller and the Stones in preparation for that evening's shoot. I went to

106

the coffee shop for some breakfast and to ponder the situation before telling Cupid the news. I glanced at a newspaper and the headlines sprang out of the page:

'STUDENTS RIOT ON THE STREETS OF PARIS'

I made a few calls and caught the first available flight to Paris. I had no idea of what to expect.

On arrival, Elaine Collard told me that Godard was on the street filming the students. 'What has this got to do with our film?' I asked.

'Nothing,' she replied. 'Jean-Luc cares passionately about the political situation here.' Well, I cared passionately about the very few days we had left to shoot the Rolling Stones. Their six days had started, and if we didn't use them we would have to pay penalties and even miss the recording. Godard was persuaded, eventually, to fly back to London, just in time.

Brian Jones, meanwhile, had been in a drug-induced depression for some weeks. He was also due to be tried by jury for a recent drugs bust. Brian's answer to the problem of being ostracized from the band, and watching things being done without him, was to go for the drugs and booze. He would sleep wherever he found himself, which was more often than not in the back of his Bentley, guarded by the Stones' driver, Tom Keylock. I noticed that Brian's fingers and hands were blotchy and swollen a lot of the time. It was sad to see this brilliant musician struggling to do things that he had been master of only months before. Brian had taken to coming back to my office, where he'd sleep for hours on end on my Thea Porter cushions, his diet seeming to consist solely of drugs and pork pies, which his faithful driver would deliver with the obligatory bottle of HP sauce.

The last day of shooting was 4 June 1968. The combined crews of the film and the recording session, plus the Rolling

Stones, assembled at Olympic Studios to record and film a version of 'Sympathy for the Devil'. A serpentine figure-eight dolly track had been laid on the floor of the main studio. The Ariflex camera had been fitted with a special giant spool, big enough to hold film to shoot the whole track in one take. Godard had been planning this for days. Charlie Watts had laid out all his ethnic drums on a Persian carpet in the middle of the studio.

I arrived with Brian, who had been sleeping in my office. He was not in good shape. He had had a row with Mick and Keith. I really felt for him. He was on his own. Meanwhile, Marianne Faithfull, Anita Pallenberg (Brian Jones's ex-girlfriend), Michael Cooper the photographer, Iain Quarrier, Jimmy Miller, all the Stones and sundry others had assembled. Godard and his crew were setting up their equipment. Marianne, Anita, Iain and Michael had been commandeered to sing backing on the 'woo-wooos' and were busy rehearsing in a booth.

It was time for action, as the filming of what is arguably the greatest rock and roll track ever recorded got under way. This atmospheric song bounced off the walls of Studio One. From the first note to the last, Godard's camera never stopped turning as it was pushed on its tracks around and around the studio, picking up Keith here, Mick there, Charlie and his drums. Up past the booth, Marianne and Anita went 'woo-wooo'. Brian's guitar solo screeched into the track, while Keith's riffs crashed. 'Please allow me to introduce myself,' sang Mick, and around and around roved the camera to the thump of Charlie's backbeat. It went on like some manic anthem, and then it was all over. '*Coupez*,' cried Jean-Luc.

There was a feeling of exhaustion and exhilaration in the studio but before anyone could relax, one of the celluloid filters in a ceiling light spontaneously combusted, setting fire to the ceiling. A dozen fire-engines wailed through the streets of Barnes and suddenly a fire-fight was in full progress.

Brian was not happy. He felt that he had not contributed to the track. It is possible that he was not even plugged in, and that Jimmy fed a pre-recorded solo into the general cacophony.

'Get me out of here, Mim,' Brian said.

I took him outside, where we watched the fire-fighters for a while. We walked together over Hammersmith Bridge with Brian's faithful chauffeur following at a discreet distance, jumped into the limo, and sped off to the Speakeasy.

Brian was due back in court in a few days to face a jury trial over his drugs bust. He was scared. His problems with the rest of the band were escalating. A touch of paranoia had set in, or perhaps he knew something I didn't, but he did not trust the Stones office to help him.

I persuaded William to pull some strings, and a good lawyer, Harbottle and Lewis, was engaged to defend him. On lawyer's instruction we took Brian to Mr Vincent in Savile Row and got him a smart suit, and he tried to dry out in my office for a week or so.

The day of the trial approached. Suki Potier was Brian's main girlfriend at this time. She was a quiet, mysterious girl (who had survived the car crash that killed Tara Browne). Suki helped Brian through the pre-trial dramas. He left on the morning of the trial in the silver Scala Brown Rolls-Royce, dressed in his new suit instead of his usual crumpled velvet gnome's costume. I received a phone call three hours later. Brian had been found guilty of possession of dangerous drugs and was sentenced to nine months in Wormwood Scrubs. This was a tragedy that Brian was in no mental condition to handle, as the letters I was to receive from him would prove.

Even the might of the Stones office could not get him off. After his eventual release, still very depressed and more or less ostracized from the band, he took to living out of the back of his

Bentley. His entire wardrobe consisted of crushed velvet items crammed in the boot.

Brian had several drivers and had grown distrustful of Tom Keylock, who worked for Keith. The story goes that one day he and Suki waited outside the Scrubs for the next inmate to be released. Soon a man came through the gate carrying his bundle of possessions under his arm.

'Can you drive? Do you want a job? You're hired. Get in.'

I never knew where Brian was when not asleep in my office. He used my place as a bolt-hole, and I just presumed that he didn't want to go home. I felt an enormous sadness for Brian at this time. He was getting more and more fucked: by the Stones, by drugs, by his own paranoia. This was the guy who a year before was strutting the world as a psychedelic superstar with his friend and wizard Jimi Hendrix at his side. On the street, these two were more powerful icons than Keith and Mick, or John and Paul. The Stones and the Beatles were business, and, of course, they were music as well. But Brian and Jimi transcended business. They were the embodiment of the Pan-like minstrel from any age, even more so when they were dying. Sure, we were all dying, but they were doing it with a little more urgency.

In mid-June 1968 I agreed to promote a small tour for that wonderful singing junkie, 'If-I-Were-a-Carpenter' Tim Hardin. One of Sybilla's directors, Terry Howard, persuaded me to bring him to London. I didn't need convincing, I loved his records. But rumour had it that Hardin was unreliable and very smacked out. Howard called me from New York and said that he had got assurances from Tim's agent that he was clean and ready to work. I put together six gigs and an opening concert at the Albert Hall, and had been told that the band would only need a couple of days' rehearsal.

I took William's Rolls to the airport to meet the band.

110

Five strung-out junkies shuffled through Customs. They had 'bad colds'.

'Hey, man, we gotta score.'

I was not into smack at the time and did not know where to get it at short notice. So I drove the sorry crew to the Cumberland Hotel and cancelled the evening's planned rehearsal. The theatres were booked, the posters up, and my artist couldn't sing a sneeze. I called Jimmy Miller, told him my problem, and like a good soldier he sent me a bag of Chinese rocks by cab. Somehow I nursed Hardin and his band through the next two days.

I learnt that Tim had found his pick-up band in the basement of the Chelsea Hotel and that they had never played together before. The two rehearsals I managed to get them to were awful. The big night came. I had promised Johnny Gilbert that Family could open the concert, their big chance to promote their first album, *Music from a Doll's House*.

Suddenly it was showtime. On went Family, but I had a problem: no Tim. The concert was sold out. Family had played their set of half an hour, and there was still no sign of our minstrel. Family could not believe their luck, and the crowd loved them, thank God. Gilbert graciously allowed them to play another set, while my scouts scoured London's smack-alleys looking for the man.

Tim arrived an hour late, out of it. Loads of black coffee and a hot shower seemed to wake him up a bit. We called Family off the stage and the Tim Hardin Band went on. The first song was played so badly, it was embarrassing. I walked onto the stage with a stool for Tim, and told the band to get lost (out of the corner of my mouth, of course). I sat Tim on the stool, and asked him to play his set solo. He pulled it off.

The next day Tim was so fucked up that I had to put him in the Priory for ten days. Naturally, the rest of the tour was cancelled. To this day I still love the bastard's records.

*   *   *

The next few weeks were full of suspense.

Godard was editing *One Plus One* and none of us knew what it was like or even, for that matter, what it was about. The only clues I had were gleaned from Godard's request for an actor with a good voice to do a substantial voice-over on the soundtrack. He sent me over a transcript of what he wanted said: an incomprehensible diatribe of blasphemous anti-papal claptrap interlaced with political rhetoric. He had used the band to express a rather confused political idealism, and this depressed me. I sent Sean Lynch down to meet Godard and read the script.

Alan Klein had replaced Sandy Leiberson as the Stones' adviser on all things. One of his first moves was to clear the decks. Our film was not a Rolling Stones production, and this annoyed him. Like Colonel Parker in relation to Elvis, Klein was now in a position to control all Stones output, be it music or film. I received a call one morning at six.

'Hello, Mim Scala?'

'Yes, who is this?'

'Freddie, Mr Klein's assistant. Mr Klein would like to have breakfast with you at eight o'clock at the Park Lane Hilton.'

After a very short preliminary at the Hilton coffee shop, he told me that he managed the Stones exclusively, that the deal for them with Cupid would have to be re-negotiated and I was not to talk to the Stones. I left in shock. It was early in the morning and I'd had a late night at Sybilla's. I called Michael Pearson and warned him of Klein's intentions. Fortunately, Michael and Iain had the experienced film producer Norman Spencer working with them. Despite several aggressive approaches from Klein, Cupid held on to the film.

But the film suffered. Godard became very possessive about it, and most of the post-production went on in private. Unbelievably, Godard had not included the complete soundtrack of

112

'Sympathy' in the film. Cupid were horrified, took control and did a small editing job on the end credits. The whole soundtrack would now play the film out.

The film was to be screened on a rainy night (30 November 1968) on the banks of the river Thames, site of the British Film Festival. Iain Quarrier went on stage to explain the new edit. He was half-way through his speech to the assembled crowd of film buffs when they were treated to the sight of an enraged Godard, who raced down the aisle and onto the stage. Before anyone could stop him, he threw a right to Iain's jaw. The public fist-fight between Godard and Iain was blown up by the press, which probably helped Cupid to make a distribution deal with Warner Bros.

I saw the film and found it depressing. I'd had such high hopes for the project, and envisioned the ultimate rock 'n' roll movie. Instead, it was scrappy and incoherent. I couldn't believe that Godard had not used the entire, glorious take.

Chapter Nineteen

I was getting increasingly frustrated with business. The stakes were getting higher and higher, and so was I. At the age of twenty-eight I was the head of an ever-expanding agency. The next phase of development was going to be a big one. Already feelers were coming to me from the industry, with hinted-at offers of take-overs and/or agency positions. I even discovered that I was on the head-hunters' shortlist along with David Puttnam for a position as UK head of Twentieth-Century Fox. The writing was on the wall for me. I started to feel a certain loss of control. It was impossible for me to just walk away from something that I had spent so much time and energy creating. But I wanted a different life. I wanted to travel, I wanted to be creative for my own sake. I was ready to commit business hara-kiri. The time had come for me to move on, or to stay and fight for something that I did not really want.

Erica Raphael, who was a friend of my secretary and girlfriend Amanda Sturge, used to come by the office at closing time to join us for a bottle of champagne. On one occasion she brought a shy, dark young man with her, who carried a guitar. After a while he played a few tunes. He was brilliant. One song after another fell out of him. He had the most magical, innocent voice, big dark eyes, a shock of black curls, and an intense personality. He called himself Cat Stevens. I called Chris Blackwell and told him that I was leaving the business, and had one last artist for him to look after before

I went. I arranged a meeting. Chris loved Cat's songs and agreed to sign him to Island Records. Cat had already had a couple of false starts in the business, and these had left him disillusioned; he was a deep young man with a lot churning in his head, and his only release at this time was his music. There was no outward sign of the changes he would go through in the next decade – his conversion to Islam and name change. I asked Chris to tie up a deal with Barry Krost, and that was the last piece of business I instigated for the Confederates Agency.

I departed with very little. I lost my file, in which was my signed contract with William, the many letters Brian Jones had written from prison, and a few other important documents. William was keeping a low profile at this time and was probably getting bored with the business. It had become serious now, and was not so much fun. It was also losing money: the offices were far too grand for the size of the business.

I cleared out overnight, and spent the next month or two in my flat in Hyde Park Gate. It became a crash-pad one could drop into at any time of night. Brian and Jimmy would often plug into my Selmer twin Zodiac thirty and jam. Jess Downs and Heavy Jelly, Stewart Levine, Hugh Masekela, and of course Bennie Carruthers would drop in and hang out. My flat was rocking.

It was 1969. Donald Canmell and Nick Roeg started shooting *Performance* in the house next door, so my flat became a hang-out for some of the players, the waif-like Michèle Breton and the silver-tongued David Litvinoff.

Patty D'Arbanville was also part of the scene. Patty was a bright, pretty little thing without a care in the world. We had a fling and then Cat Stevens fell in love with her, and wrote his great song, 'The Lady D'Arbanville'. Meanwhile, in my flat a real version of *Performance* was going on. Benito Carruthers was staying in the back room with the tragic Henrietta Guinness.

Brian Jones was deteriorating fast; his relations with the Stones had bottomed out and he had split with Suki.

I was so pleased to have my freedom and no telephone – I had ripped that out. I was reading Huxley, Hesse, Freud, Jung, Gurdjieff and Ouspenski, and had become very interested in hallucinogenics. The mad professor Michael Hollingshead acquired a sample of pure LSD 25 from the Sandoz laboratory and we were busily trying to work out the ultimate dose. He'd changed Timothy Leary's life by turning him on to it.

Brian Jones was working on putting an album together from the recordings he had made in the Moroccan hill village Jajouka. Listening to the trance music of Bou Jeloud made a big impression on me. I couldn't wait to go off in search of other master-musicians in Africa. But how could I find them? When Hamri the painter had met Brian in Tangiers and driven with him into Jajouka, Brian had no concept of what he was about to witness.

The festival of Bou Jeloud involves the sacrifice of a goat or goats and the skins are then used to dress a member of the Jajouka sect, usually a young boy. Then, with a constant and steady build-up of music, the boy becomes entranced and transforms into Bou Jeloud or, as we call him, Pan. As this ancient, animistic fertility rite unfolds, the women of the community are menaced and chased by the apparition, scattering in terror as their fertility is reaffirmed. The ceremony and the music continue throughout the night to the throbbing drums and the incessant wailing reeds of the rhaitas. Eventually, Bou Jeloud retreats, the boy comes out of his trance and all returns to normal in the village until the next year.

Could we find the master-musicians of other sects? We made a pact that one day, God willing, we would go off in search.

I decided to go to North Africa by myself, although I was falling to pieces. Had I done the right thing? I had seen a lot of the real world, if you can call show business the real world.

116

Frankly, it stank. Only the creative were clean; the rest, the lawyers, the managers, the accountants, were there for the ride, and usually they got the best seats. I was one of them, and I didn't want to be. I would have to be creative if I was going to survive.

Chapter Twenty

I disposed of all my immediate ties in London, renting out my flat to Barry Krost. I still had an on-off relationship with the lovely Amanda, who had been a friend long before she became my secretary at Scala Brown Associates. Amanda and I packed a few things into her silver Mini Minor, and with a wonderful sense of freedom we left the madness of London on a lazy, meandering drive that eventually led us down to Spain, where I wanted to revisit the village of Ojen.

When I saw it again, nestled in the hills of Andalucia, I knew that this was where, for now, I wanted to be. The white and cream houses with their flat terracotta rooftops shimmered in the heat haze. Marbella, just five miles below, the strip of Mediterranean sea, and the coast of Morocco could be seen on a clear day. We drove the little Mini into the steep, narrow village streets and parked in the Plaza Della Concepción with its old church and two bars, a bakery, a *tienda*, and charming little houses, which leaned against each other like loving brothers.

It was 1 February 1969. Marbella was just one of a string of delightful village resorts that ran along the coast like a necklace from Malaga to Algeciras. We rented a small house in the centre of the village. The surrounding mountainous countryside was beautiful; a profusion of sweet-smelling herbs were beneath our feet as we walked the dusty hills and always the cooling breeze wafted up to us from the sea. It took me no time at all to forget about my past life as a whiz-kid agent.

Our social life revolved around a small family hotel called La Fonda. It functioned as a meeting-place, post office, and general sorting house for the expatriate community. There was plenty of space in those days, even at the height of the tourist season, and everybody knew everybody. Life was blissful without telephones or a business to worry about. I could paint and write and become a complete hedonist.

Prince Hohenlohe bought a chunk of land on the beach and built the Costa del Sol's first exclusive club hotel, the Marbella Club. Marbella became the 'in' place for anyone cruising the Mediterranean in a yacht. So my life became one long party yet again. Bob Ho arrived in a new Mustang Mac. 1. He had with him the psychedelic Bradley Mendelson. Bob invited Amanda and me to drive to the Algarve, where his father, the Tai-pan of Macao, had a huge house. So Amanda, Gavin Hodge and I followed Bob and Bradley on a stoned drive to Portugal.

On the first night Bob, Bradley and I dropped some acid and drove into town to find some music. We must have looked a sight. Bob wore skin-tight silver thigh boots and a psychedelic shirt, topped by his flowing mane of black hair. Bradley and I looked equally bizarre cruising the conservative Portuguese streets in our throbbing convertible. When the acid took over we parked the car and fell into a nightclub. After an hour or so of tripping to disco lights and music, we were arrested and frog-marched into a police van and chucked into a cell. We must have seemed very strange to our captors under the bright ceiling light. We had no idea why we had been arrested, and our captors had no idea that we were connected to the Honourable Mr Ho of Macao and Hong Kong.

It emerged that we were suspected of being Angolan spies. (Portugal was at war with Angola at the time.) We dropped a mandrax each and slept like babies on our hard bunks. In the morning Gavin arrived with a lawyer and our passports. A very embarrassed police chief apologized for arresting the son of Mr Ho.

About this time I received a letter from London telling me that Terry Howard (who had assured me that Tim Hardin was clean as a whistle) was to marry Miss Venetia Cunningham. Venetia's mother was on her way down to organize the wedding for a hundred or so guests at the Marbella Club. She came to see me in Ojen.

I suggested a more romantic alternative: my village. A lovely traditional bedroom could be made up in many of the houses. In fact, I would try to take over the entire village for the wedding. That meant virtually sealing it off from the outside world and populating it with all the wedding guests. All food would be made by local women, all the bars would have free tabs on the wedding day. The village could use the income, and the cost of the party would be significantly less than that of an orthodox affair. Mrs Cunningham discussed the idea with Terry and Venetia and it was decided that I should attempt to organize it.

My first job was to convince the mayor and the community committee that the idea was not crazy. The logistics were intimidating. There are laws in Spain that Franco instigated during the Civil War which forbid meetings of more than ten people. Special licences were needed from Malaga. Next I examined all the houses; the owners agreed to make one room in each house available and suitable for a foreign guest. The best linen and traditional Andalucian decor made the rooms charming. I then made deals with all the bars in town and worked out the menus. The local priest took care of arranging the wedding ceremony. The Marbella Club, however, was not happy that a huge party had been deflected from them. This made me somewhat unpopular. I started to get visits from the bureaucracy. Then the fire and safety people came at me. The Guardia Civil made themselves very busy, but I had already

120

acquired the public meeting certificate from the council in Malaga. The Guardia Civil was paid off and promised to cordon off the village to anyone without an invitation.

Guests were due to arrive from all over the world. Amanda floated around the house, spacing out as she prepared. Johnny Gilbert and Leigh Davis arrived in an E-Type on speed, and then half a dozen Harley Davidsons drove in the day before the wedding: my good friends Johnny Gaydon and David Enthoven (managers of T. Rex and King Crimson), Esmond Cooper-Keys, Emma and Annie from the King's Road. They set up camp on the roof of my house with a good supply of Moroccan kif. They hung out while I finalized things. Finally I crashed out exhausted, well satisfied with all my efforts.

I was awakened early the next morning by a loud banging on my door. I went to the window to see a crowd of familiar locals and the priest. I noticed another crowd looking down at us from the road that ran along the top of the village higher up the mountain.

'*Buenos dias*,' I said cheerfully to the padré, thinking he and his friends had come to start the celebrations in some obscure Spanish way. But the reaction to my cheery good morning was not what I had expected; in fact it was distinctly hostile.

I threw on some jeans and, followed by Johnny Gilbert, I went down and opened the door. There was the priest, the mayor and the chief of the village council. Roughly translated, they said, 'Emilio, this is very grave. It is not possible that this should happen in our village. This is a great scandal. We will have to cancel the fiesta.'

'What is the problem, padré?' I asked.

The priest cast his eyes to the ground and then stood back, looking up at my roof. Looking down were my friends from the King's Road. We could only see them from the waist up and they were smiling down at me without a care in the world.

'Hi, man, this is fantastic. What a scene, man.'

121

I gave them a wave and got back to the serious business of interpreting the bad news I seemed to be getting. Alejandro, the one-armed veteran from the Civil War, stepped forward. He had a great sense of humour and spoke army English.

'Emilio, your friends are fucking like goats on the roof. The whole village has been watching them.'

Then he repeated what he said to me in Spanish. Alejandro only had one voice and it was loud. His remark broke the ice and the assembled crowd broke into roaring laughter. I looked up and there were my naked friends in blissful oblivion. After much talking and a donation to the church funds, I apologized and sternly rebuked my mates. The crowd dispersed and several hours later the guests started to arrive.

The wedding went off without a hitch. The Guardia Civil were true to their word and fearlessly repelled all would-be gatecrashers. The village of Ojen turned into a carnival. A troupe of flamenco dancers from Granada danced the night away, small bands of guitar-playing gypsies played beautiful music under the pepper trees, the sangria flowed, and Terry and Venetia's wedding was a total success.

I became increasingly restless after the party. Eventually, Amanda returned to London, something I wasn't ready to do. I moved into the guest cottage at La Jumita, the beautiful house of Dandy Kim's charming and generous ex-lover, Sara Skinner.

Sara had fallen in love with Kim shortly after the 'Warner Affair' scandalized Riviera society. In 1953 headlines in the British papers announced that Scotland Yard and detectives from Interpol were searching for Dandy Kim, the charming ex-public school playboy and amateur jockey. Jack L. Warner the movie mogul had claimed that his safe had been robbed of the equivalent today of half a million dollars in cash. The finger of suspicion fell on his future son-in-law, my old friend Kim. The tycoon's beautiful teenage daughter Barbara and Kim had been an item on the Côte d'Azur for some time. Queen's Counsel was briefed. On legal advice, Kim did not return to France to answer the charges; Napoleonic law would have had him banged up for years while he awaited trial. Three years later the trial was eventually held in France *without* him. He was found guilty *in absentia*, sentenced to serve four years and ordered to repay the half million dollars. Failure to do this would increase his sentence by two years.

Kim, refusing to recognize the right of the court to hold a trial without him, did not appeal, and was given another year for his impertinence. Meanwhile he had opened a nightclub and water-ski school in Tangiers, as a front for a smuggling operation to Spain and Italy. He was actually running cigarettes and whisky in a souped-up motor-torpedo boat. But Interpol became alerted when he and an associate orchestrated the meeting in El Minza when the king of the London underworld, Billy Hill, handed over power to the new kings, the Kray twins. Again the law was too late. With the help of the villains, the Dandy escaped on his MTB to Algeciras with a hold full of hooch! Seven years after the robbery Kim's luck finally ran out. The perseverance of the French authorities, backed by the power and political influence of Jack L. Warner, paid off, and in 1960 while recovering from concussion received from a nasty fall in a steeplechase at Newbury, Kim was arrested. Bail was set at an incredibly high twelve thousand pounds, and put up by his old school friend Lord May and his lover, Sara Skinner. True to form, Kim continued to delight the press by riding in races in between his Bow Street appearances.

Inevitably extradition came and in 1960, Kim began a five-year stretch in the high security wing of the prison at Fresnes. It got worse before it got better for Kim. He was transferred to the infamous La Maison Centrale de Poissy, a hard man's jail. Then the strangest thing happened. Jack L. Warner informed the French authorities that he had been advised on matters of which, he declared, he had not been aware when he had accused Mr Waterfield. The fact was that the safe had contained cash and certain documents, one of which was a damning screenplay penned by the Duchess of Windsor's ex-best friend, the American party-giver Elsa Maxwell. It must be presumed that the revelations in the screenplay would have been a major embarrassment to the Duke and Duchess, and would almost certainly have jeopardized the movie mogul's treasured social connections. According to a William Hickey article in the *Express* in May 1998, the 'Maxwell Memoir' dealt with the clandestine birth of a love child to the Duchess.

After a very unpleasant fourteen months in La Maison, Kim was mysteriously released and hastily deported on the undertaking that he keep a forty-year embargo on any information he may have gained from the Warner safe. To my knowledge Kim, like the Pope with the third secret of Fatima, has faithfully kept his secret to this day. Kim, who readily admits to a wicked past, has always vehemently denied any part in the burglary, though he has hinted that the key to the Warner mystery was that the safe was opened twice. Sara loved Kim and hung on until his release. It then became obvious that the relationship was over. Heartbroken, Sara moved to Marbella, and threw herself into creating La Jumita, an old-style Andalucian villa, with soft colours, clever rustic plasterwork, terracotta tiles, a pool, and my cottage hidden in a lovely garden surrounded by chiramoa trees. There I lived throughout the autumn of 1969 and into the winter of 1970.

Word reached me that Jimi Hendrix had joined Brian in heaven. They were burning up like moths in candle flames. Brian had died on 3 July 1969. He had an asthma attack in the pool, couldn't reach his inhaler, and drowned amid high speculation. It was such a waste. We'd talked a couple of weeks before about him coming to Morocco. Jimi died on 18 September 1970; Janis departed on 4 October 1970, and Jim Morrison was to die a year later on 3 July. They left behind a treasury of sounds.

I spent that winter by the log fire writing my first novel. The word was out in London that I was having a great time in Spain, and old friends started to arrive. Gavin Hodge came down with his wife, the heiress Jane Harries. Jane had bought a Jensen Interceptor for cash, but could not drive it, so she flew me to London so that I could drive them to Spain. Gavin decided to make the trip à la *Easy Rider*, on the new chopper that powerful Pierre had built for him. Jane and I had a fantastic drive across France and Spain. Gavin was supposed to arrive right behind us. Two, three, four days later an exhausted and bedraggled Gavin crawled into the house on a totally fucked chopper. 'Fuck that *Easy Rider* shit, man.'

The village started to fill up with other crazy expatriates. Art galleries, bars and restaurants began to open, all owned by friends. I was not earning any money, the summer was approaching, and something had to be done. I took the ferry across to Morocco and bussed up the Rif Mountains to Ketama to find a good smoke. I bought some jewellery in Quazazate, and then began scouring the markets in the villages I drove through. Although I didn't have a lot of money, what I did have I spent on jewellery, desert silver and coral. Back in Marbella I had no problem in selling the things I'd bought for a profit. I had found a nice way to make some cash.

Michael Pearson was taking a Mediterranean cruise on his new yacht, *The Hedonist*, along with Willie Fielding the artist, Patrick Lichfield, and George Lazenby, who had just finished his one and only performance as James Bond. Michael invited me to join the party for the rest of the cruise. Naturally, I accepted. In Tangiers the crew managed to find a berth for the huge yacht right under the medina walls, and Willie and I took a trip around the medina on small motorbikes belonging to the yacht. In the Petit Socco I almost ran over a beautiful young girl wearing a full-length, antique, white lace wedding-dress. She didn't notice the near-miss, so I stopped the bike and followed her into a pharmacy. She couldn't speak French and was trying to buy toothpaste. Willie and I offered to help her out, and soon she was on the back of my bike.

We rode to Achmed's famous boutique, which was to a pot-head what a visit to the caves of Chateau La Tour would be to a wine connoisseur. His little door made itself known to us in the maze of alleys and we entered a dark corridor opening into a small room, the walls of which were hung with interesting arabesque bric-à-brac, all of it for sale. Achmed had profited from visits by the Rolling Stones and their friends, and his stock had improved since my last visit.

He was a wiry little man with a shock of wild hair not unlike the Jimi Hendrix poster he had sellotaped to one wall. On the table were the quintessential Moroccan tea-glasses and a small radio tuned to Cairo. He wore a special hand-woven, multi-coloured *djellaba* from the Rif Mountains, and welcomed us with a glint in his eye. He ordered tea by raising four fingers to someone through the open window and proceeded to dart about bringing us nice things to look at. Then he took a seat. He produced a two-piece *sebsis* pipe, studded with semi-precious stones, and an ancient leather kif pouch with a few long, thin chains attached. From the chains at two- or three-inch intervals hung baubles as on a charm bracelet – exquisite, strange little things.

He filled his *sebsis* or kif pipe from the pouch, lit it, took a couple of hits to get it going, and passed it on to Willie and me. Achmed waited, watching the pipe's effect on us. 'Kattama goo, zero-zero, chocolaté,' he chuckled.

We sat there poleaxed. This was powerful hash. We bought some after several pipes. Before we left his den, Achmed rooted around in his magic drawer and produced a cellophane-wrapped lump which he pressed into my hand. 'Chocolaté,' he whispered. We eventually got out, and sat with a first-class hash high on the Socco steps watching the wonderful sights of Tangiers, until we were straight enough to get back on the motorbikes.

I fell in love with Virginia on *The Hedonist*. We'd disappear for long periods while Michael played backgammon with Jess Down up on deck.

Jess, an exceptional painter and a Lee Marvin look-alike, was a good friend of mine. We found him having an enormous row with the Moroccan Customs. I strolled over to the scene.

'What's happening, Jess?'

Jess had done one of his flips. 'Fucking Customs. I've got a truck full of Glaoui tat I'm taking to London for Gibbs, and these arseholes want to charge me to take the fucking shit out of the fucking country.' He was in full rant: 'They should fucking pay me for doing them a favour. It's only tat anyway.'

Gibbs was Christopher Gibbs, whom Jess worked with in London. The Customs men cleared him just to stop the tirade, and I brought him back to *The Hedonist* to join the party.

We stayed in Tangiers for about a week taking excursions on the bikes into Fez and the Rif Mountains. I was buying new stocks of jewellery as well as goofing about. It was then I realized I wanted to live in Morocco. Tangiers fascinated me – what this little city must have seen over the millennia, sitting at the mouth of the Mediterranean. *The Hedonist* eventually dropped Virginia and me off in Marbella. She moved in, and we spent the winter together in blissful idleness.

Chapter Twenty-one

Virginia and I returned to London the next spring. I introduced her to Jose Fonseca, who ran Models One. Jose signed her up. She started to work immediately. But I had itchy feet and was dying to get back to Morocco. With a lot of help from Michael, I put together a long-wheel-based Land-Rover, equipped with sand-ladders, a winch, spares and, most importantly, a Nagra tape-recorder. It was a carawagon conversion which could sleep four comfortably, and I had it fitted out like a mini-house with everything I might need for an extended exploration of the Atlas and the Sahara. I named it *Shadowfax* after Gandalf's horse in *Lord of the Rings*.

The King's Road was changing fast. The influx of Carnaby Street stores made it feel synthetic now. Edina Ronay had given up acting in favour of fashion and her boutique, along with Peter Golding's emporium Ace, was now dressing the glam-rock glitterati. Alvaro's was gone, and the new place to hang at was the Casserole, presided over by the charismatic Dickie Kries and his bevy of camp waiters.

A few awful things had happened since I had left. In August 1969 Charles Manson had murdered Roman Polanski's beautiful wife Sharon Tate. At the time Michael Pearson and Iain Quarrier were in the Californian desert shooting the last scene of their film *Vanishing Point*. From the mobile production office Michael called Sharon to invite her to the end-of-shoot party. Sharon was eight months pregnant with Roman's child and begged off coming. It took longer than expected to shoot that last scene. It was nearly eleven o'clock when Michael and Iain finally drove into Mulholland Drive and past the compound where the Polanski house was. They decided not to disturb Sharon with a phone call as it was late, and drove directly to the *Vanishing Point* party. As the party wound down a couple of blocks away, dawn broke over the Polanski household and the Manson massacre. Michael heard the chilling news on the radio as he drove away from his party. Had he and Iain dropped in on Sharon, they too would have been victims of Hollywood's most evil murder.

Not surprisingly, Michael and Iain took the whole thing badly. Iain never fully recovered, nor worked again as an actor or producer. When I last saw him, rock climbing in the Lake District, he was handsome as ever, but a different man.

Dear William Pigott-Brown's property company with Michael Taylor had been floated on the stock market; the shares were peaking, the property boom was on. So confident was William of this lucky streak that he signed personal guarantees for more acquisitions. It looked like William had made it, big time, as shares in London Bridge continued to soar. Then came the crash, and the bottom fell out of the property market. William suffered a major wipe-out.

I was ready to leave London again. I drove up to see my parents in Forest Hill. Hamilton Lodge, the gothic Victorian house my grandfather had bought after winning the Irish Sweepstake, had been sold. My grandmother, Uncle Joe and Dad bought three houses in London Road opposite the Horniman Museum. Since I was a child I had run around this great Victorian philanthropist's collection. Old Mr Horniman (of the tea family) built the museum to house his collection of ethnic weapons, musical instruments and African and Oriental art. I knew the place like the back of my hand. As I walked around, I realized that

129

I remembered all the things in the mahogany cases from my childhood: American Indian items, tomahawks, spears, beautiful hand-crafted bows and arrows, Mongolian artefacts, Tibetan and African carvings. The musical instruments department to this day probably houses the most comprehensive collection of ethnic instruments in London. There was a large pair of iron castanets in the North African department which had always fascinated me as a kid. I never knew what kind of noise they made or even how they were supposed to be played, but they looked like foot-long, flattened dumbbells. I was to meet the men who played those very castanets on the journey I was about to make.

Dad was not well. He looked pale; he had never really shaken off the jaundice he contracted in Burma during the war. Mum told me he had a heart problem, which he wouldn't mention himself. A couple of days later, he went into King's Cross hospital for a bypass (an operation still risky in 1971). I went to see him in hospital and we had a long chat, the first we had had for years. I talked about my intended trip to Africa. He had difficulty understanding how I could afford to take off without a job or any visible means of support, and my appearance as a fully fledged hippie didn't help. Then we started talking Land-Rovers; he had been a sergeant-major in the REME, a branch of the Royal Engineers. He helped to build roads and bridges from Chittagong to Kashinaburi, cutting through impenetrable jungle, coping with mosquitoes, fever, rotting sores and deadly Japanese booby-traps. This made my comfortable sojourn into the Sahara sound like an afternoon tea-party.

We had a good laugh. I suspect he knew that he wasn't going to make it out of hospital. I discovered from my mother later that Dad secretly loved my adventures, and kept my photos and cards in his desk.

He had always worked hard to keep things together. He

gambled too much, and played a mean game of snooker – he was the west London champion two or three times. I was leaving in a couple of days. He seemed relieved when I told him, and laughed at my suggestion that I stay until he came out of hospital, telling me in the dry way he had to send my mother a postcard.

I left London in *Shadowfax*. I had no plan, no time restrictions, a few quid in my money belt, and green-card insurance from the AA. And a quest to follow. I was going to Morocco to find the master-musicians and record their music. Marbella was, of course, the first stop on the journey.

All the old faces were still there but the place was growing fast. I had only been away six months and already there were new developments springing up. Three new hotels had laid foundations and what had been a charming beach with a few shacks was now one long row of breeze-block restaurants. Signor Bannus had finished his Marina Porto Bannus, complete with its own village. For me, Marbella had been ruined, and it was going to get worse. I drove the Land-Rover into Gavin's garden. My plan was to sort out the contents of my new mobile home and prepare it for my journey to North Africa. I laid out all my possessions on the grass so that I could see what I had and what I might need. I popped an eight-track tape into the player. 'Purple Haze' came whacking out of my souped-up speakers.

'Hi, Mim. Where you going, man?'

It was Ollie, a dubious character from San Francisco.

'Morocco. Tomorrow,' I replied.

'Well, you need a snort of this,' whereupon he offered me a toot from a little bottle. I took one, and one to be civil, thanked him, and got on with my chores.

Ollie left. 'See you, man.'

I decided to change the tape. I picked up *The Best of Cream* and slipped the big cassette into the player. I then fell out of the

Land-Rover and lay spread-eagled, unconscious on the grass. I had no time to wonder what was happening.

An undeterminably long time later I was travelling at terminal velocity through the universe, bathed in green light, with my feet in a pair of cosmic stirrups heading towards Arcturus or some such star. Sparks were flying off me like a comet's tail. Slowly the sound of Jack Bruce's bass came through the hallucination, and voices that weren't on the Cream track. 'Close his eyes,' somebody said.

I came to slowly in a very comfortable bed. I looked around me when I could to discover that I was sharing it with Roger Lewis – I'd know his woolly head of curls anywhere. I turned, and there on the other side of me was Gavin Hodge. The dreaded Ollie had done us all up with a whacking dose of pure Angel Dust.

Apparently, I had lain in the garden all day with my eyes wide open. Roger was sitting in a beach café when Ollie's drug hit him. As for Gavin, he had gone to pay his rent to his sweet little old landlady, and got struck down in her kitchen. A sensible girl had rescued us and put us all to bed. I had to postpone my trip for a week while the optical effects in my brain wore off.

A few days later, I bade farewell to my friends in Marbella and drove down to Algeciras and onto the deck of the *Ibn Battuta* with a huge smile on my face.

Chapter Twenty-two

As the ferry chugged out of Algeciras harbour on its short cruise across the Strait of Gibraltar, *Shadowfax* secured to the prow deck, I felt intense excitement watching Andalucia diminish and the Rif Mountains loom up ahead. From the dock in Tangiers I could see the souvenir touts massing at the foot of the gang-plank, ready for the tourists to disembark. The first thing to hit me was the mixed scent of herbs and spices, mint and harbour detritus.

I drove my Land-Rover off the ferry, and was directed by Customs officers to a shed where a load of hippies were waiting in line. The Moroccan authorities were implementing one of their periodic crack-downs, part of which compelled hippies to have their hair measured, and, if necessary, cut. A refusal could result in access being denied. I was questioned as to the purpose of my visit, while my traveller's cheques were counted and papers checked. The officer in charge fingered my shoulder-length ringlets. 'You must cut your hair,' he said with a hint of sadistic pleasure. I was sent into a room with a mirror, table, pair of scissors, and several other hopeful hippies, some of whom were trying to tuck up their hair to make it look shorter. One old hand asked me if I had more than a hundred dollars on me. I told him that I did.

'You'll have no problem, man. Just cut half an inch off and he'll let you through, but if you don't have money the bastard will make you cut it real short.'

This was not a good start to freedom on the road. I cut a minuscule snip off my hair and went back in. The officer looked at me as I held out the lock in the palm of my hand. He couldn't have been nicer; he gave me my money and passport and waved me through. The hippie who had advised me was outside about to be sent back to Spain. I asked him how much money he had and gave him thirty dollars to bring his total above the magic hundred.

'Cool, man.' He thanked me as he rejoined the queue of hopefuls.

Within a week I knew my way around Tangiers and could weave my way through the narrowest streets and alleys. In the evenings I would drive out to Cap Spartel where under the cliffs a colony of hippies were living in makeshift tents made of plastic and driftwood. At night communal fires were lit on the beach, and travellers would gather to smoke kif and watch the sunset. I spent days wandering around the various markets that exist in Tangiers, especially the shanty dwellings and stalls of the Thieves' Market on the edge of the Socco Grande, where one could buy all manner of merchandise. Hill-people from villages in the Rif Mountains would collect there, hawking their hand-woven *djellaba*, thick knitted socks, leather crafts, cheeses, fruit, and bread baked on the spot in clay kilns. The Thieves' Market was aptly named. You could buy anything there: jewellery, electrical goods, even stolen European cars. Another section of the market housed the *tiendas* of the artisans, shoe-makers, potters, lamp-makers, knife-grinders.

I met my first friend here, Sidi Abdelkader, sharpening knives at a stonegrinder. He was a gnome of a man with a ready smile and a knitted wool hat on his small head. I found him working away on the blade of a knife. I stopped to watch, fascinated. He looked up, aware of my presence, and smilingly asked me in Spanish if I would like some mint tea. We were soon chatting over a *sebsis* or two of his excellent kif and delicious tea nanna.

On a tray in his cubicle was a collection of beautiful Arabian knives, silver-handled, curved-bladed, some bejewelled. He explained that at the festival of Howli the male head of every family had a duty to buy and sacrifice a sheep for his family and that the knives had to be sharpened. He laughed when I told him that it was my intention to find the master-musician of Morocco.

Nightlife in Tangiers revolved around the cafés in the Petit Socco and the Socco Grande, or, if one preferred, the more elegant cafés of the French quarter in the boulevard Pasteur. I would hang out in the medina and kasbah, listening to music, drinking tea and smoking kif. Whenever I heard music being played I'd gravitate towards it, until I found all the cafés where musicians played. Often my search was rewarded by remarkable musical encounters with a maestro of the lute, or the bindir drum. Sometimes I'd be lucky enough to hear a very different sound emanating from the depths of the kasbah. When this happened I'd try to find the source, but usually to no avail; the music would disappear behind high walls or a maze of alleyways. I would then sit in the street and listen for hours to some magical audio ceremony out of sight and reach, and have to settle for the remnants of the sound that drifted over the rooftops. Here was the music I was searching for, and it was not played in the cafés. It was very specific. The main instrument was a type of bass guitar, the gimbri, played by people called G'naoua.

I got to know the Rif and Atlas Mountains well over the next year. The Land-Rover's four-wheel drive enabled me to follow mule tracks, some of them far off the nearest roads. They led me into a different and beautiful world of remote mountain villages. While the twentieth century and all its advancements were evident in Morocco in the late Sixties, up in some of these villages ancient customs and rituals as old as time were still in place. Tombs of local saints were always deeply respected, and most had a day assigned to them for a festival of some kind. A village called Sidi Hiti, some fifty miles from Tangiers in the Rif, housed the tomb of a saint of that name, apparently a wandering Dervish who had arrived in the village several hundred years ago from Afghanistan. He lived by the river and told the villagers to put all leftover cous-cous into the river that ran nearby so that the fish could feed. The fish soon grew large and fat. Sidi Hiti would sit by the river and smoke hashish, which he taught the villagers to make. He then instigated a cooking fire in the centre of the village and said that anyone who asked would be fed. Over the years the word spread; soon all manner of wandering holy, and not so holy, men came to Sidi Hiti to eat and smoke hashish with the sage.

I learned where to find the weavers of the best *hiak* (a wool cloth highly sought after in the cities) and where to find the best leatherwork, embroidery, pottery, as well as tailors, carvers and hashish-makers, but the best musician still eluded me. I had recorded hours of music on my little Nagra recorder by many musicians who claimed to be G'naoua, but I was still a long way from sitting among the master-musicians of this sect. The search was pleasant, driving from place to place on a hunch, or following a tip gleaned around a fire in some remote mountain valley.

Shadowfax was well worn in by now. If I wished to stay in a village for a week or more, I would attach a great tent that I had had made to the rear end of the truck. This gave my vehicle three floors in effect. The Land-Rover had been converted into a carawagon by a company in Slough, and its flexible aluminium roof could be raised with the aid of concealed collapsible walls. Under this extended roof two sturdy canvas hammocks could be slung. From there you could look up at the stars through oval windows set in the roof. This was the penthouse suite. Below this was the main floor with the travelling seats, which could

The Three Musketeers: *above*, Mim against the artists' wall at the Confederates Agency, *above right*, Iain Quarrrier at Cupid Films, *below*, The Hon. Michael Pearson, during the pre-production of Jean-Luc Godard's Rolling Stones film *One Plus One*, May 1968. (*Dick Polack*)

Above left, The Family at Sybilla's. *Above*, Dolly girls with Tony Hicks of The Hollies. *Left*, DJ Kenny Everett with Tony King, John Peel and Johnn Bonding; Rob Townsend and Jimmy Miller. *Below far left*, Johnny Gilbert and Bob Reisdorf, head of Liberty Record *and left*, Mim, Sir William Pigott-Brown, Iain Quarrier and Harry Baird. 1966 (*London Life*)

Left John Lennon and George Harrison at Sibylla's, 1966.

Right Brian Jones, a Stone alone, leaves Sibylla's opening party. (*John Seymour*)

Below Mick Jagger and Michèle Breton, in the bath during the filming of *Performance*, 1968. (*Dick Polack*)

Below right Mick Jagger on the way up, Brian Jones on the way down, during the filming of *Rock and Roll Circus*, December 1968. (*Dick Polack*)

Mim joins the flamenco dancers at the Howard wedding at Ojen, Marbella, 22 August 1969. (*Venetia Howard*)

Newlyweds Venetia and Terry Howard, with Amanda Sturge, at the wedding feast. (*Venetia Howard*)

be rearranged to form a comfortable double-bed. There was a sink with running water, a stove, and a small refrigerator built into cupboards. The storage space was well designed and held all of my recording equipment, tools, and most importantly, the Land-Rover *Royal Engineers' Manual* and handbook, which allowed an idiot like me to fix anything that went wrong.

I always took a lot of trouble in selecting a perfect spot to park when evening came, carefully aligning *Shadowfax* so that the landscape, sunrise, sunset and moon-view could be seen clearly. Usually I made camp on the outskirts of a village, or simply in a beautiful place. If I wanted company I would turn up the sound and play some of the recordings I'd been making. This attracted the children, who would come to giggle and look curiously at the crazy hippie and his Land-Rover. The brave ones would talk to me in pidgin French. After the kids, the local lads would appear in their best mountain *djellabas*, and I would invite them to sit at my fire and listen to the music. The *sebsis* would invariably come out, and we would compare kif, each man being proud of his personal blend; the pipemanship of the Berbers is a sophisticated art.

There are several points of etiquette involved in the communal smoking of kif which an infidel had to learn if he wished to achieve a modicum of respect.

Berber Kif Etiquette
Never refuse a *sebsis*.
Don't slobber all over the mouthpiece.
Don't mess with another man's scuff (small clay bowl) or clean it out.
Always smoke to the end and discreetly blow out the dead ash (this requires perfect timing; if the ash gets cold it won't blow out of the scuff).
Never claim that your kif is better than your host's.

If you must cough, take your host's *sebsis* from your mouth.

Always pass the *sebsis* back to your host.

If you are going to be sick, or are about to spin out, take a walk.

If you are offering a *sebsis*, always light it beforehand.

If your kif is crap, don't offer it.

Never ask for a *sebsis* (patience will prevail).

After a few months, I could speak a smattering of Berber which, combined with my bad French and slightly better Spanish, allowed me to communicate. I was by no means the only traveller. Like the monkeys who all learned to wash potatoes on the same day, hundreds of young people had climbed into Volkswagen buses and hit the road. French, German and American hippies were on the move, but my vehicle allowed me to be more adventurous than most. I had no problem exploring off the beaten track. After the Rif, I started on the Atlas Mountains, weaving my way through passes from Fez to Marrakech, Todra to Ifni, Tizi-n-Test to Oukaimedan. I travelled alone most of the time, but if I met someone I liked we would travel together for a bit. I built up a network of interesting places to stay or stop over. I would get to what I thought was an inaccessible mountain village and find a gang of French hippies living in a kindly sheik's goat shed, smoking twenty chillums a day and dropping acid at every sunset.

I would run into weddings and feasts of different kinds, stop to watch and be invited to join in. Whenever this happened I'd hang out with the musicians and, if it was warranted, would bring out the Nagra. If I heard something amazing, I would stay in the vicinity for a while, trying to find out who had taught the musicians to play. Occasionally someone would give

138

me the name of a man or a place. In this way I continued my search. Camping on the outskirts of a village and playing my Nagra recordings always worked; the music would attract the children, then their elder brothers would follow, question the music and tell me of any musician in the village who played such and such. Then they would come out to see me and, if I was hospitable enough, they would play for me into the night around my campfire. Those nights were wonderful – high up in the Atlas, the moon drifting in the Arabian sky, a flute, or a lute and drums – all-night raves with much eating of hashish and smoking of kif.

Apart from diesel for *Shadowfax*, I needed little money. Vegetables and good bread were cheap in the mountains. I soon learned to use cumin, turmeric, and all the market spices in my cooking. There are good trout and barbel in the Atlas streams and rivers, and whenever I spotted likely water I would enjoy a spot of fishing.

I decided to venture down to the edge of the Sahara. I meandered my way through Ouarzazate, and down to Goulimime and Tan-Tan, which was the last outpost of Morocco proper in those days, and therefore the last place to stock up on needed goods. Tan-Tan was a tax-free zone and full of traders from all parts of the Sahara. Camel trains came from Spanish Sahara and Mauritania, and huge red Ford trucks from as far as the Hoggar in Algeria, and Timbuktu. Toureg and Bedouin traders swapped merchandise – sugar, salt, cloth, cigarettes, electrical goods and, the thing that interested me, *le bijou*, the jewellery of the Sahara people.

My collection started with a dozen Toureg silver rings, beautiful things with strips of different-coloured enamel embedded in the silver. As time went by I bought anything I liked the look of, and I soon had a good knowledge of what was real and what was tat. Before I realized it, I had several bags full of silver, coral, amber and amasonite jewellery, all of it authentic and

139

most of it antique. It had a lovely rough quality, the stones and amber polished by years and years of being worn by working women. I bought other items as well, anything small, pretty, old and well made.

I now had two quests to follow: the search for the music, and the penetration of the network of Sahara *bijou* traders. Every kasbah, even deep in the Sahara, had a money lender equivalent to our pawn-brokers, and I was soon trading with men from Goulimime to Erfoud and even farther south in the kasbahs between Tata and Mahamid. I bought what I could until my cash was too low to continue investing. I was hearing lots of music, some of it really good, but I was looking for Paganini.

Low on funds and no nearer finding my master-musician, I decided to drive back to Europe to see if I could sell some of my jewellery. On my way north through Morocco, I stopped in the eucalyptus forest of Deibet, near Essaouira. The ancient remains of the palace of Mogador were there in the forest, now a broken ruin and overgrown with vegetation. I found a beautiful spot with a magnificent view of the Atlantic, where I set up camp, built a fire, and got the tagine pot going. I put up the roof of *Shadowfax*, whacked up the sounds, and settled down with a chillum to watch the sunset.

Then I saw what looked like the three witches from *Macbeth*. One of them approached me, and producing a few vegetables from somewhere in her black skirts, asked me with a Californian accent if she could put them in my pot. Always pleased to have a bit of female company, I told them that my tagine was nearly ready and that they were welcome to join me. Just then I caught a very unsavoury whiff. I checked to see if it was me. But it was definitely human waste. Then I noticed that the three girls were filthy. Their arms and faces were smeared with shit. I didn't fancy having them dipping into my pot or sitting too close. I noticed other moving shadows, coming out of the forest in ones and twos. Some sat a respectful distance from my camp

140

but within earshot of my sounds. A few others came closer armed with sticks and wood and sat by the fire, adding fuel to it. The newcomers weren't smeared like my first visitors, but they were far-out radical hippies who looked more like a bunch of serfs from the Robin Hood era.

As the fire-dwellers started to put chillums together for the sunset, the fire grew and soon I was in the middle of a beach party. Then a small red-haired, bearded man, naked except for a genuine pigmy lap-lap, walked up accompanied by three boys, one of whom carried a very large water-pipe. The naked one introduced himself.

'I am Robin, the leader of these people. You will smoke with me, yes?'

He was an Albanian who had been living in the Cameroon jungle for three years with pigmies and had taken a pigmy wife.

With great ritual Robin's helpers produced the paraphernalia that went with the giant water-pipe. The base of the thing was a fired earthenware bottle with a capacity of about two litres. The bits were made of bamboo and the chillum itself was a carved ebony Kathmandu special. Robin sat cross-legged by the fire, while his faithful young acolyte passed him what he needed to fix a smoke: a sharp knife, a piece of linen for the saffi, and a large, diabolical-looking lump of red Lebanese hash on a wooden board. This was not the inferior Moroccan hash that most of the hippies smoked. One of the kids went down to the river to fill the jar with fresh water while Robin worked away on the board rubbing up a smoke. By the time he'd finished he had in front of him a pile of mixture that would have filled two tea-cups, half of which he ceremoniously rammed into the chillum, muttering, 'Bomshankar, bombulay.' He fixed the chillum to the rest of the pipe, then took the mouthpiece saying, 'We smoke and then we talk.'

I remember thinking that if he expected me to smoke that

chillum out, I wouldn't talk for a week. I could tell by the smell that came off the board that Robin's hash was the real thing. One of the acolytes lit a fan of seven matches. Robin woof-woof-woofed at the mouthpiece until billowy clouds of fragrant smoke engulfed us both. On a dopeless night in London I would happily have settled for the peripheral taste I was getting just by sitting there. Robin did not stop puffing until the pipe was smokeless. He took the chillum off the pipe and smacked it upside-down on the board, producing a mound of fine ash. This he blew into the night air. He immediately refilled the pipe with the remaining mixture. Smiling in the way that only a very stoned person can, Robin pushed the pipe to me.

I looked around at the faces at the fireside. The shit-covered girls and their mates looked back at me. I had got myself into a dope duel with Billy the Kid. I examined my opponent's face. He was fucked up but definitely not gone. I reckoned that a quarter of an ounce of dope plus four Gitanes had gone into the mixture. I also reckoned that if the dope didn't do for me, the Gitanes probably would. A fan of matches exploded into flame and I lit the pipe. I took in great lungfuls of sweet smoke. Eventually I too took out the chillum, tapped it on the board and blew the ash away. I stood up, climbed into the *Shadowfax*, put on Santana's *Abraxas* and then went into a wonderful hash hallucination.

Robin was rubbing down again and very soon was sucking at his second pipe. I didn't much like the look on his face. A smidgen of paranoia crept over me. This guy was manic. Was he really Billy the Kid disguised as a pigmy, and did he want to kill me? Fortunately, proceedings were cut short when Robin puked violently into the fire and spun off to lie down in the sand. I would have done the same if I had hit the second pipe. Instead, I lay back and slipped into a wonderful hash crash.

When I awoke in the morning, Santana was still going around and around on the eight-track. I was covered with a blanket, the fire was alight and the three witches were bathing in the river. I lay there watching them. Unclothed and clean, they were unrecognizable: three wholesome, attractive young girls. They came out of the water and back to the fire when they saw that I had stirred.

'Hey, man. Do you have any coffee in your truck?'

They were giggling and laughing and naked. One of them in particular was very good looking.

'You look and you smell a lot better now than you did last night.'

They all laughed. They washed their clothes, made coffee and explained that they were three middle-class San Franciscans who had only been in Morocco for two weeks and had caught a bus from Tangiers to Deibet for no particular reason. The bus journey was at night, so they had seen nothing of Morocco except the forest of eucalyptus and the palace of Mogador. They didn't trust Robin and his gang, so to prevent rape and sexual harassment they had come up with the idea of smearing shit all over themselves. I asked if it had worked and they laughed and said that even covered in shit a couple of freaks still made passes at them.

They moved into *Shadowfax* and we explored the Atlas together for a few days before I dropped them off in Tangiers to catch a plane home. I checked into the Atlas Hotel for a couple of days, to take a proper bath, and make a few phone calls. One night, while walking back to the hotel from the Petit Socco, I heard music coming from windows high up in an old fortified building in the kasbah. I pulled up the hood of my *djellaba* and sat in a doorway close by and listened. The rhythms and tone of the instrument that led the music was like a bass guitar. It was special. I had heard something similar in Marrakech but nothing of this intensity.

My Nagra was in *Shadowfax*, which was locked in Mohammad's garage. I walked back to the boulevard Pasteur, but the garage was shut. I went back to the kasbah to listen to more of the music, even if I could not record it, and spent the next hour looking for the alleyway I had sat in. There was no sign of the alley or the music.

The next morning I went down to the Thieves' Market to have a chat with Abdelkader and told him my story. He laughed. 'Things like that happen in Tangiers. At least you have had your proof, *inshalla.*' He was right. I now knew exactly what I was looking for and that it was in Tangiers.

It was time to sell jewellery again, so I left for Marbella. Before I knew it, I was selling necklaces to the Hollywood hippies at the Marbella Club for vast profits. A third of my collection went very quickly, easily making back my investment.

Chapter Twenty-three

I set off for London with what I had left. When I arrived, I sadly found out that my dad had died. I had missed his funeral. This made me very sad. I was delighted we'd had a proper talk before I left. I went straight home and stayed with my mum for a fortnight. Eventually I sold the jewellery to a dealer in the Chelsea Antique Market for a nice profit, and set off once more on my quest. I had left instructions with my Sahara dealers to save things for me, and they knew exactly what I was looking for. I made a fast drive down through Spain and caught the ferry for Tangiers. I worked my way around Morocco, going down through Fez to Erfoud and then to Tinerhir, re-investing my profits as I went.

A dealer in the Todra Gorge had a fabulous collection of silver, coral, and turquoise. He was a particularly hard man to bargain with. I would go to his large house, which was in a mud-built kasbah that was hundreds of years old. The ground floor of this fortified desert building was given over to goats, donkeys and a superb Arab stallion, his pride and joy. To enter his domain it was necessary to pass through the stables and climb the chunky, baked-mud steps to the next floor where it was cool and sparsely furnished, and mostly given over to the women and children. Up a further flight of stairs was Lacien's Aladdin's Cave.

Lacien was a short, round man with a hennaed beard, who kept an embroidered leather bag full of cash around his neck and a silver dagger in his belt. I would visit and eat with him every day as he produced box after box of trinkets. Negotiation was a slow process. He knew I had more money and I knew he had more treasure. I like to think he enjoyed the haggle as much as I did; he was an old fox and a worthy adversary.

Lacien had two sons, bound for college in Casablanca, who were sometimes allowed to sit in on the negotiations. His wife and daughters, in bare, tattooed, hennaed feet, would pad across the carpet as they brought in tea, freshly baked bread, *zibda* and honey in that generous Berber way. Lacien had learned that I liked to smoke kif (which he thought made you crazy) so he always had a good supply, reckoning that it would make it easier to blow my mind.

His timing was always perfect. He would pad over to one of his trunks or cupboards and bring back a bundle of something fabulous to tempt me. 'I just show you this, it is much too expensive for you.' In this way the pile of purchases grew, until I had spent my earmarked cash. At the very end of this negotiation he produced a set of beautiful silver bracelets from Madagascar, set with coral and turquoise and rough, but sound, enamelwork. I clearly could not afford these unless I put back a lot of items from my pile of purchases. He had told me earlier about his sons, so I decided to try my secret plan. My mother had given me a large suitcase with all my Sixties clothes – suits from Dandy fashions, John Crittle's amazing tailor shop, and a pink gabardine suit from Sharks with braid piping around the jacket and down the side of the trousers. Now that I was on the road I would never wear them again.

I told Lacien that I had two beautiful suits in the latest London fashion that would fit his boys. Their eyes lit up. I went down and brought up the suitcase. I opened the case with a flourish and produced them. Even I was shocked: they were outrageous. I told Lacien how much fashionable suits like that would cost and offered them to him in exchange for the

Madagascar jewellery. The boys were instructed to try them on. Mrs Lacien and the daughters were watching and giggling through the half-open door. They were dressed in the fashion of the Moroccan Sahara, layers of cloth, brightly coloured gauze over satin shifts, all bound together with five metres of red goats'-wool cummerbund.

The boys looked a sight in their swinging Sixties outfits, but they were delighted. Lacien was not convinced. He wanted another four hundred dirhams. I couldn't afford this unless I took some of the jewellery from the pile. I told the boys to take off the suits and opened the suitcase as a bluff to see a pair of psychedelic Carnaby Street boots, calf-hugging ones that came to just below the knee, with very high platform heels and a zip up the inside. They were made of multi-coloured pieces of scrap leather sewn together in a patchwork.

Mrs Lacien appeared. She grabbed the boots and put them on, to shrieks of delight from her daughters. The zips didn't quite do up, as her calves were too thick. I smiled at Lacien. He was a beaten man. There was no way his wife was going to give those boots back.

I set up a stall at the Saturday market in Tan-Tan, spreading out a few enticing bits of jewellery on a red felt rug, hoping to attract a trade or two. I was thrilled to be sitting in the market with my Sahara scarf wrapped around my head, believing that I was indistinguishable from the rest of the traders. Suddenly I caught sight of a pair of extremely shapely ankles in extremely inappropriate high-heeled shoes. My eyes climbed up the legs and body to the face. It was Virginia. I had last seen her with Polanski in London.

'Hello Mim,' she said. 'I'm on a photo shoot for *Paris Match*, and I suggested the dunes for a location.' She was with her photographer, Bernard Mignon. I was delighted to see them and took them to my camp in the dunes where we spent a couple of days grooving. Then I drove them to Marrakech to catch their plane. Virginia was a lovely girl. I was glad she had found a career. I was no good to her at this time. I was busy.

I drove to Tangiers via Marrakech and up to Oukaimedan, which even in summer retains a good fall of Atlas snow. *Shadowfax* climbed the mountain pass without difficulty until we met a blocked road. As I turned around, I heard a voice calling from a Land-Rover and small caravan parked there.

'Hello, GB.' It was a middle-aged English woman. 'Would you like a cup of tea?'

Soon I was sitting comfortably in the caravan, having tea and animal biscuits with this couple. The old gentleman was slightly put out at the state of me with my ringlets, bangles and beads, but he took it in his stride. He sat in an armchair in front of a gas fire, reading a week-old copy of *The Times*.

'I love mountains,' he said. 'Any chance we get we head for the great hills, don't we, dear?'

'We do,' she responded, offering me another biscuit.

'I'm a retired magistrate,' he told me. 'The name is Barroclough.'

I asked him if he was the same Mr Barroclough that used to preside over West London Magistrates Court.

'How did you know that?'

'Because I taught you how to make free telephone calls.'

He looked at me over his half-moon spectacles. 'Emilio Scala,' he said. 'You're quite right, you did teach me. Do you know I tried it out, as soon as I had an opportunity, and it worked.'

We drank tea until it was time for me to drive down the mountain to Marrakech.

My next stop was with Rocky and his Swedish wife in the hills outside Agadir, where they lived in a shack near the cascades. Rocky looked like Charles Bronson from the left

148

profile, and the Phantom of the Opera from the right. He had caught the blast from a malfunctioning napalm grenade in Vietnam and not surprisingly hated war. His skills as a mechanic were well known to the trucking fraternity in Morocco. He could fix anything and had saved many a Volkswagen bus from an undignified roadside death. Scattered around his shack were the metal carcasses of ones he'd failed to save, whose spare parts filled wooden boxes. Rocky could have been a prototype for Mad Max. He was totally self-sufficient in his hillside camp and ran a shanty hotel for the travellers who waited while he fixed their trucks, while his wife Lilly cooked an evening meal for anyone hanging around. Rocky always had the best smoke and conversation. It was a pleasure to pass a few days with him and his family. Soon I was heading for Tangiers with a European tour in mind. Where could I sell my cargo?

My first stop off the ferry was, as usual, Marbella where I refreshed myself before the long smooth drive through Spain to France. I was as free as a bird, with money in my pocket, my *Shadowfax* to sleep in wherever I liked, and a sackful of Saharan treasure to trade for cash, my only company the occasional hitchhiker and my sound system.

I approached St-Tropez from Aix-en-Provence. I found a secluded beach a few miles from the town and set up camp for the night. It had been a long drive at a maximum diesel-speed of fifty miles an hour. I slept like a log and awoke at dawn, to see a beautiful, calm sea reflecting the golden rays of the sunrise. I noticed a speedboat offshore cruising very slowly in circles, and could just make out three people in it; whatever they were doing had a ritualistic, surreal quality to it. The boat cruised around slowly for a long time. After a while I drove into St-Tropez. It was a wonderful fishing village in those days, with discreet little hotels and pensions, interesting bistros and cafés lining the waterfront. In the grand villas scattered through the hills and along the private beaches were the playgirls and

149

playboys of the Seventies: Günter Sachs, Brigitte Bardot, Johnny von Newman, Agnelli, Victor Barclay, Onassis, Niarchos, Sam Spiegel, Ricky von Opel, Mohammad Al-Fayed and his young son Dodi. I parked outside Les Escales and found *The Hedonist*. Within minutes I was in the middle of a great reunion of old friends from the King's Road. It was lunch, dinner, party, nightclub, the sack, sunrise: an endless round. After months in the Sahara this suited me just fine. Everyone wanted one of my silver and amber pieces. My jewellery became that season's major fashion item.

One evening I strolled into the bar of Les Escales and a crazy German guy called Ricky grabbed me: 'Mim, let me introduce you to my sister.' Ricky introduced me to a petite girl named Putzy, with beautiful eyes and a perfect body. I put my arm around her shoulder.

'You're just my size,' I said.

I had received a message that day from Jimmy Miller. He was living with the Rolling Stones in Cap Ferrat and had installed a complete recording studio in a huge old house, where they were producing *Exile on Main Street*. That night Putzy and I were in *Shadowfax*, driving along the Grande Corniche with the Stones blaring from the mini-Tannoy speakers. We were on our first date. A hippie looking like a Saharan gypsy, travelling with a young maiden in a Land-Rover caravan, amidst bells, incense, and rock and roll.

We pulled up at the house in Villefranche. Eventually two little boys in Indian war-paint came to the gate.

'Who are you?' they asked.

'I'm Mim and I have come to see Jimmy. Who are you?'

'We are Tommy's sons.'

'Is your daddy here?'

They ran off and returned with Tommy Weeber, a handsome Stones hanger-on with a penchant for smack, who hung out with Keith and Anita. He opened the gate. There was always a prickly vibe between the acid heads and the smack heads, as if each group knew something the other didn't.

The house was full of musicians: Jim Keltner, Jim Price, the Stones and Bobby Keys. The Weeber boys and Keith and Anita's son, Marlon, played around like Medici cherubs. Jimmy took control of the session, which stopped and started at the whim of Mick or Keith. Putzy and I spent the night grooving to the sounds. The sun eventually rose and we had a communal breakfast with nannies and other characters who appeared from various corners of the house.

Over the following weeks Putzy and I became inseparable, living in *Shadowfax* up in the hills around St-Tropez. She told me that her father had recently died and that she had sprinkled his ashes on the waters of his beloved bay of Canubier. It turned out that this was the strange boat ceremony I had witnessed from the beach, a little cosmic coincidence that seemed to cement our relationship. After a couple of weeks living rough in *Shadowfax*, she announced that I should visit her family house in St-Tropez. We skirted the old town and drove down a long lane, lined on either side with giant bamboo, and there we came to a high wall with a tough wooden door. Inside was a manicured garden that dropped away to a magnificent Fifties pink stone house, with a tower and private port beyond. Boats bobbed in the calm, blue water. We walked down the steps through the garden to be greeted by a big-bosomed woman in a white housecoat, with rosy cheeks, a pile of flaxen hair, and a smile full of flashing teeth.

'My dear where have you been? I've been so worried about you. Come, you look terrible. You must have a bath and eat something.'

Putzy laughed and introduced me to Lorna, her surrogate mother. Lorna grabbed us both and soon we were in a bathroom with Lorna and the spaniel Vania, having our clothes

151

confiscated. That was the beginning of the most wonderful summer of my life.

We spent the summer in this magical environment, with full use of the toys that the house had to offer. My favourite was *Batman*, the sleek Riva Super-aquarama speedboat, whose twin engines could cut through the Mediterranean like a knife through butter. Our visits to the Stones became more frequent. Now we would go by sea, cruising along the Cote d'Azur to Villefranche. Putzy and I both loved the water and spent hours in boats. This story nearly ended on one of these trips.

We had taken the Riva along the coast for the Stones' end-of-album party. We hung out all night listening to tracks and horsing around with Bobby, Jimmy, Keith, Mick, Anita and Tommy Weeber, his two sons and Marlon running naked through the grounds. Some French Keith clones had infiltrated the party and were busy trying to impress with their drug-taking prowess.

Putzy and I climbed aboard the Riva to return to St-Tropez at four in the morning. The stars reflected off an inky lapis-coloured sea, and there was no moon to speak of. Bobby, Jimmy, Keith and company waved us goodbye, I revved the engines and cast off into the night. The cruise home usually took about two hours at full speed, as we kept the lights of Nice, Cannes and Juan Les Pins on our right and took a straight line to the lighthouse of St-Tropez. At full speed in the semi-darkness, the wind rushing through our hair, we grooved to the sound of the twin engines and the swoosh-swoosh of the waves as *Batman* cut its course.

About half an hour out of Villefranche a dark shape loomed up in front of us. I throttled back as hard as I could, but it was too late. There was a great whump, the boat shot into the air, and landed with a mighty crash back into the water. We were knocked over but unhurt. I engaged the engines and turned the boat around slowly. Putzy manned the spotlight and searched the water. Suddenly, but gradually, the giantic head of a cashalou whale emerged from the inky black a yard or so away from us. A solitary eye reflected the spotlight beam. Putzy was upset that we might have hurt the magnificent creature. Then the huge fish dived and resurfaced lazily, waving its tail as if to tell us all was well.

We continued our journey and after a while felt an ominous change of wind on our faces. I could no longer see any lights, a mist had descended and the sea was stirring. The Riva, designed for Italian lakes, was about to take on a fully fledged mistral, whose sudden appearance could transform a smooth silent sea into a boiling cauldron. I carefully accelerated up the walls of the waves, and decelerated to glide down them, trying desperately not to be swamped in the troughs. We had lost all sense of direction, the wind howled and whipped us with salty spray, the stars had gone out and we only had a half-tank of gasoline.

I was too stoned to be scared and held a straight course for St-Tropez. As it got blacker and blacker, the mistral roared and it seemed that we were in Hades, climbing to crazy heights and slipping into endless troughs through the darkness. We were both exceptionally calm, and I felt like Captain Ahab after Moby-Dick. After what seemed an age, the mistral subsided as suddenly as it had come, and dawn produced an impenetrable grey fog in which we drifted to the sounds of King Crimson. Slowly an islet, topped by a stone-built tower like that in a Tarot deck, loomed out of the mist. I manoeuvred the boat into the little dock and we heard voices as two fishermen appeared probing the rocks for octopus with long barbed spears. Somehow we had landed on the Isle de Port Crios, miles past St-Tropez, almost opposite Marseilles. We were soon chugging into the comforting private port of Tour de Voiles, where Ricky and a party were already on deck drinking Bloody Marys.

*   *   *

153

My true love, the open road, was beckoning. *Shadowfax* was fed up with tarmac beneath its wheels. Putzy and I headed back to Spain. I stopped in Marbella to introduce my new partner to the gang, who all agreed she was lovely. Putzy was very mature. She had an insatiable curiosity for all things spiritual; she was an avid reader, and had a wide knowledge of esoteric philosophy. She had unusual energy and could walk for days, ski and water-ski; after I taught her to drive, she was far better than me on long hauls. I was in love probably for the first time in my life.

We left Marbella and were soon trucking down to Morocco. It was her first trip and she adored it. I was looking for the G'naoua. I still had not heard their music played in the context of a ceremony. My quest became centred on looking for people who had been rid of possession or cured by a shaman. Such rituals were accompanied by appropriate music. But these events were sacred to the local people. Why should they discuss deeply personal matters with anyone, let alone a curious hippie whose motive for seeking the information could be spurious? We trod lightly. We continued to discover the culture of the Moroccans: their food, customs, family life and folklore.

After a while, inspired by Hesse, we decided to travel east. I gave the key to *Shadowfax* to my Cousin Ronnie and told him to come and take it for a drive into Morocco. He did this, and Putzy and I went up to St Moritz. We stayed there for a couple of months, walking the mountains and exploring the secrets of the Engadin. There are small hidden lakes in the mountains that held stocks of wild trout. I set about learning to catch these, which required me to master fly-fishing. One day, flailing away on a small secluded lake, I believed that I was alone, but feeling eyes on me I turned to see a dapper individual in hiking outfit shaking his head at me. I thought perhaps I was fishing on private water.

He approached me. 'Here give me your rod,' he said in an Italian accent.

He took off the fly and tied a piece of wool from his hat to the leader. I met this man every day for a week. His name was Charles Ritz, one of the greatest fly-fishers of all time. Under his guidance I became a match for the Engadin trout. In this beautiful place Putzy and I planned our journey to the East.

At weekends a gang of Putzy's student friends from Munich would drive up to visit us. A few weeks before we were to leave on our journey, the Munich gang came up, driven by a guy called Michael, who crashed the car in Celerina. The following weekend Michael crashed yet another car. Again, no one was hurt, but I didn't like Michael. He was quite different from Putzy's other friends. These weren't simply unlucky accidents; the guy was reckless, and he didn't give a shit. Still, we all had a lot of fun. As the season in St Moritz was peaking, Putzy and I left. We had travelling to do.

Chapter Twenty-four

We flew to Bombay and then travelled through India and Pakistan. We were as free as birds, and we loved it. After a month or so we heard from Ricky, who wanted to come out and meet us for a holiday. We arranged to meet him in the Seychelles, at a house we had rented on the island of Mahé. On the plane from Karachi, I got talking to a German boy who was on the last leg of a world tour. He was going to have a rest in the Seychelles for a week or two. He mentioned that he had a small lump of excellent hashish (as did I), so we arranged to meet on a desert island beach to compare our smoke.

Putzy, Johann and I disembarked from the plane in the newly built Victoria Airport. I went through Customs first and waited for Putzy. She came through. I called a taxi and asked it to wait. I asked Putzy if she had seen our companion. Apparently, he had been just behind her in the Customs queue. A man came over and flashed his badge. He was English with a west London accent. He asked me if my name was Mim. I said it was, pushing my lump of dope down the back of the taxi seat and asking Putzy to wait in the cab.

'We have a guy in there who would like to talk to you. We have just busted him for smuggling.'

I looked at him and tried to make friends. 'What's he smuggling?'

'Hash,' he answered proudly.

156

'How much?' I asked. The copper showed me a marble-sized lump.

'Surely not,' I said. 'We're on a desert island, for God's sake. What harm is he going to do? This boy has just travelled around the world on a shoestring, and now he lands in paradise, a thousand miles from anywhere, and you want to bust him for a marble of hash?'

He looked at me, one west London guy to another. 'Nah. I don't like him. He's German and a dirty little bastard; he's got loads of nude photos of his girlfriend in his bag.'

'What are you going to do with him?' I asked.

'He'll appear in court tomorrow morning, get sentenced, and probably do six weeks until he gets deported. Come on. He wants to see you.'

I went into the office and there was Johann. He seemed okay and I told him we would do what we could to help. Johann was led away. With a snide smile, the copper told me to enjoy my holiday. I went out, got in the taxi, told Putzy what had happened, and retrieved my lump of hash from the back-seat crevice.

We arrived at the court house at nine o'clock the next morning, as instructed by the copper, to find it empty. I asked a cleaner when the court opened. 'Oh it's all finished for today. There was only one crime and he was found guilty.' I discovered that Johann had walked into court at eight-thirty, pleaded guilty, and been sentenced to a month's labour in the Seychelles Prison, where they cut off his long hair.

We rented a car and drove to the prison up in the hills. The islands of the Seychelles archipelago are fauna- and flora-filled jewels in a turquoise sea. Johann was not allowed a visitor on his first day. The governor, a Maurice Chevalier look-alike with rum on his breath, was charming and treated us as if we'd come to visit him from Europe. Trapped as a prison governor in paradise, he had obviously gone a bit crazy himself. Though he was more interested in chatting up Putzy, he eventually told us that we could bring in food, drink, cigarettes and money for our friend, and waved us goodbye like a hotel manager. We took supplies up every week, but were never allowed to see Johann.

Travel agencies hadn't found the Seychelles yet, so it was still a remote ex-pat haven. My hero was a man who had come to the islands in the Forties from South Africa, bringing with him a fortune in syndicate money and a copy of the last will and testament of the famous pirate Babous, guillotined in Paris in the early nineteenth century. Before dying, Babous apparently drew a cryptic map with clues to finding the treasure based on the twelve labours of Hercules. I met this man in a bar in Victoria, where he was living in a shack with several women and countless children ranging in appearance from ginger Irish to jet black. He used to dream of Babous and claimed to meet him often in the night to discuss clues. 'He knows I have him beat, that's why he comes to me. I will find the treasure. It's chess, my boy, you see. It's chess.'

When he had first arrived on the island, he had employed hundreds of Seychelles workers to dig for him. The first dig unearthed a battered statue of Andromeda, whose broken finger he thought was pointing to the treasure. Some five years later, having dug through a small mountain, he ran out of money. He raised a second fortune, but this too was spent. But he was absolutely sure he had now cracked the mystery.

We finally managed to broker Johann's release by promising to take him directly to a plane. We picked him up at the prison gates. He looked fantastic: fit, healthy, with a deep tan, 'No problem,' he said. 'I've had a great time. I've worked in a mountain plantation, chained to a murderer who was a very nice guy. We had fish curry and rice and fruit every day. I couldn't have found such an experience anywhere else in the world.'

He thanked us, and climbed aboard his plane.

Putzy and I booked a flight back to India with a stopover in Sri Lanka. We were stunned as we flew over Serendipity, as the island was once called – from the sky it looked incredible. On landing in Colombo we went straight to the British Embassy to apply for visas. In the lobby there was a blackboard where someone had written, 'Film at three o'clock: *The Underwater City* by Arthur C. Clarke and Michael Wilson.' It was five to three. I walked into a room with a few lines of chairs and a projector and screen.

'My God! It's Mim. What took you so long? Come and watch our movie.'

It was my old friend Michael Wilson. Rumour had it that he had come to Sri Lanka as a steward on a passenger liner in the Fifties, had jumped ship and stayed in Colombo, earning a living diving for lobsters. During his underwater work he had stumbled on a previously unknown ruined city in fairly shallow water. His discovery came to the attention of Arthur C. Clarke. Michael took a local wife and had lots of children, while he and Clarke collaborated on projects.

Both of them were interested in science and mythology. Clarke had invented the communications satellite, among other things, and had begun to write *2001: A Space Odyssey*. Michael is credited with a lot of the esoteric undertones that pepper the book. Clarke was once asked if he had patents on the communications satellite. He said no. When asked if he regretted this, he replied, 'What would I have done with a hundred billion dollars?'

Michael helped us with our visas and took us back to his house where we met his family. In the back of the house was his study, stuffed with books on mythology, comparative religion, diving and archaeology. The centrepiece of the room was something that looked like a Buddhist shrine. From it he took a box, and soon we were tripping on LSD. In this condition we accompanied him on an enlightening tour of Colombo.

The next day he drove us down to Hikkaduwa, a pristine little fishing village built on a coral reef where Arthur had his house and scuba-diving business. There were four or five copra-built structures on the beach, which included a three-roomed hotel called the Coral Sands. It became our home for the next few months and its staff of three looked after us. Siri Gunawardena, a Sri Lankan gentleman determined to do well for his family's sake, owned the place. His father had been a tea planter and Siri took me to visit the old plantation in the hills behind Gall, with its wonderful teak buildings with slatted walls, where the drying crop could benefit from the crisp mountain breezes. The Victorian machinery, amazing contraptions for rolling, cutting and drying tea leaves, was still in working order. The place still smelled of fragrant tea.

Also at the Coral Sands was a wonderful old tubercular man, as thin as a pin and always helpful, Raja Singha, a reincarnation of the last king of Kandy — at least that is what I christened him. Raja Singha was a sort of innocent Zen master. His duties encompassed everything from cleaning fish for the cook to climbing tall trees for my coconuts. Raja's Zen way was to serve, and this he did with remarkable selflessness. He worked steadily and constantly. He would arrange a fresh little altar in my room every day, decorated with lovely fresh flowers and a couple of nice joints.

Then there was the cook — a beautiful, petulant Tamil boy called Ragi. Ragi cooked all the meals, which we ate communally unless we had guests, at which times Ragi, Siri and Raja Singha would naturally fall into servile mode. Nothing I could do or say could talk them out of this behaviour. I was occasionally able to turn the tables by waiting on them.

We shared our new home with Manjou, a pet monkey. He travelled between the house and the verandah via the windows facing the coral reef and the vast expanse of the Indian Ocean beyond, where evening after evening, season after season, the Indian Ocean sunset never ceased to amaze.

Inland and across the railway tracks lay Hikkaduwa proper, a scattered collection of palm-thatched houses set in a coconut plantation. Mounds of coconut husks were turned into twisted copra rope, the mainstay of the village workforce. There were several very interesting temples within an hour's walk inland. One in particular was a magnet for me. There I befriended the abbot, who let me come to meditate with his novice monks. The monastery housed all the horoscope records of every Buddhist monk in Sri Lanka, from centuries ago to the present day, hand-written on parchment and bound in decorated, carved-wood covers. These mysterious little books lined shelf after shelf throughout the monastery, where they waited to be pulled out and used as references for the calculation of the future careers of the monks. The abbot and his novices wrote with old ink pens in the most beautiful Pali script, with its loops and curlicues. Putzy and I felt ourselves to be in heaven.

The water in the Hikkaduwa reef was perfect, crystal clear, with thousands of fish, from sea-snakes to schools of yellow-fin tuna, myriad tiny reef-dwellers, multi-coloured moray eels and waving octopi, all living together in a coral cathedral whose golden columns of sunlight appeared to support the surface film. I would sometimes swim out beyond the reef into the deep water of the Indian Ocean and encounter mantas, barracuda, sharks, and the occasional big tuna that would run along the deep edge of the reef.

The sunset was always honoured, not just by us but by the whole community. Nobody was so busy or blasé that they could fail to appear for the evening ritual. The smoke of the copra fires from the beach and the tantalizing smell of frying chillies and Ragi's secret curry spices would float around after sunset.

161

As we would make our way from the reef to the verandah, a meeting-place at this time of day, Arthur would stroll down from his house to join the surfers and travellers attracted by the spices in the air. We would all eat and hang out until the early hours, perhaps make a fire on the beach, or go for a night-time swim in the reef. We were often visited by a mother turtle struggling up the beach in the warm sand. And we'd watch her as she patiently dug her nest and laid her burden of dozens of soft white eggs.

The Sri Lankan people were full of grace and had exquisite manners. The influence of British colonization, subtly adapted to a native culture and climate, was evident everywhere. The train station in Hikkaduwa had a signal-box that could have been from West Sussex; the station master, thirty-five years in service, was straight out of *The Railway Children*. But similarities with England ended there, with groves of coconut trees, snakes in the water-butts, monkeys screaming from the tree tops, and lithe women in wrap-around sarongs padding barefoot along the hot silver tracks I crossed each day for my visit to the abbot. He was a charming man who tolerated my questions about meditation and reincarnation. What with visits from Michael, chats with Arthur, sessions with the abbot, and daily lessons in humility from Raja Singha, this old Teddy boy was well locked into his esoteric journey.

Putzy and I discovered the magic of Polonnaruwa and Anuradhapura for ourselves. Every step you took in Anuradhapura revealed a carved rock of exquisite beauty. Thousands of carved stones from the palaces and temples of the kingdom of the First King of Lanka lay at our feet. A huge reclining Buddha, carved from living rock, looked down on the scene, keeping an immortal eye on the slow but sure erosion of this once-glorious city. Putzy and I spent a lot of time here, alone save for the occasional visiting monks who would enhance the

162

beauty of the place with their saffron robes and banana-leaf parasols. We travelled lazily around the island, always returning to our hideaway in Hikkaduwa to reflect on what we had seen and refresh ourselves in the reef and the healing waters of the Indian Ocean.

Unlike me, Putzy had complicated business affairs to contend with. She needed to understand the full significance of her inheritance. The time had come for her to face responsibilities and return. We took a last trip to Kandy, and said goodbye. I was deeply in love with her. She was the most interesting woman I had ever met. There was a communication between us that was magical. I put her on a plane for Switzerland with a mixture of sadness and joy.

Chapter Twenty-five

I stayed in Hikkaduwa to continue my search. Now that I was alone I meditated every day, often at the monastery. I swam for several miles each day, out in the deep water beyond the reef. In the afternoons I would write for a few hours, all the while being taken care of by Siri, Ragi, and my faithful Raja Singha.

I lived alone for the most part, except for Manjou, the white-faced monkey. LSD was taking me on deeper and deeper physical and spiritual journeys. I was reading a lot and continuing with my meditation with the abbot. He used to come to visit me at the Coral Sands on Thursdays, always arriving in the old monastery Wolseley, crammed full with novice monks, who would clamber out to spend a few hours on the beach as happy as children. After tea and a tin of Raja's biscuits, we would all swim in the reef, saffron robes billowing from my garden fence.

I would call Putzy once a week from the doctor's house up the beach. She was getting on fine in St Moritz and would return as soon as her business allowed.

One day I was sitting on the verandah at sunset, a glorious backlit monsoon sky sweeping to the horizon, when a small gecko dropped from the ceiling and landed on my bare shoulder. The little creature was so shocked that he stayed quite still where he landed. I picked him up with his heart beating as I put him on the wall next to me. He stayed for a moment and scurried away. I continued with the joint I was rolling when a second gecko fell from the ceiling. This one landed on my head, then dropped to my knee and ran off. I had seen thousands of geckos on my travels but I had never seen one fall from a ceiling. To witness two do this within a matter of minutes aroused my curiosity. Had a snake chased them out of the rafters? I had a look. No snake. I continued to ponder this as I smoked and watched the magnificent storm sky grow fierce and orange and gold.

Raja interrupted my thoughts as he brought a tray of tea and pancakes. 'Tell me, Raja, is there any folklore in Sri Lanka about geckos?'

Raja put his hands together, and wagged his head. 'Oh yes, master Mim. You must see the lizard lady in the village. She will tell you.'

After tea we both set off over the railway tracks, through the coconut grove, past the shrimp lagoon and the copra-spinners who waved at us, and along a raised irrigation ditch to a small village of five or six huts in a clearing, where chickens scratched the dirt and a couple of dogs lay sleeping with one eye open (this is the only way for a Sri Lankan dog to survive; they are not best-loved creatures in Serendipity). Raja took me to the verandah of one of the huts and respectfully called a name.

An old crone came out. Although her hair was silver it was the hair of a child, as bright as silk and shining like velvet. Raja introduced me and backed away. She invited me inside where plants grew by the door and copra and charcoal burned in a clay pot. She sat me down on the floor rug and questioned me about my geckos. What time of day did it happen? Which way was I facing? Where on my body did they fall?

I answered her questions as best I could. Then she took a ball of coloured yarn, and tied several loops of it around my index finger. Finally, she tied a knot and burned off the loose ends with a piece of smouldering copra. 'You must be very careful,' she said. 'You are in very grave danger. You must

165

not go in the sea until this ring falls off your finger. Do not worry, when the yarn falls off you will be quite safe.'

I gave her a few rupees, which she took gratefully, waving as we left.

That night I listened to the sound of huge raindrops clattering onto my corrugated roof. I fell asleep to this percussion, the drumming of the gods. In the morning the sun was shining and there was no sign of the monsoon storm. Charlie the Fish, an Australian trucker wandering the world looking for the perfect wave, came by for breakfast. He reckoned that the monsoon had brought some incredible sets with it that were hitting the beach about a mile up the coast. I loved to body surf and the thought of some good waves was a major temptation. But I refused with some feeble excuse.

The waves stayed for a week and every morning Charlie the Fish tried to get me to join in the fun. By this time the word had spread down the coast that there was great surf in Hikkaduwa. A dozen or so surfers had materialized to enjoy the waves while they lasted. I limited my sea-going activity to paddling in the reef during my daily walk. I was dying to swim, but I had paid the doctor and was now taking my medicine. The magic band of coloured thread was still wrapped around my finger forbidding me to swim. It was frustrating listening to the ecstatic surfers describe the waves as we sat around beach fires at night.

A few days later the surf subsided and things returned to normal. Most of the surfers moved on but Charlie the Fish stayed at his favourite spot, a gap in the reef which allowed him to surf in the deep water.

One day I took a lunch of buffalo curd and papaya up the beach to watch him. I was sitting on the sand, twenty yards from the sea, and saw Charlie sail through the gap in the reef. It wasn't a big wave that he was riding but he fell off. He was no more than a hundred yards from shore, but he started shouting 'Cramp, cramp', and I could see he was struggling.

Without thinking I ran down the beach and into the sea. When I got to him he was relatively calm. 'Just hold me up, man, it's my legs, man.'

I trod water and held him, thinking that I could work him to the shore. The problem was that the water looked weird. It was shimmering and the waves seemed to be vibrating rather than rolling.

'Hold on to me, man,' he said, a little fearfully. 'It's a rip, man, it's a rip.'

Before I noticed we were sucked out through the gap in the reef, and were being swept along the coast. I knew it would be impossible to swim against the current and Charlie insisted that he would be all right and was just relaxing his legs. Suddenly I had a flashback to the old lady. Oh shit! I raised my hand to look at my finger. No yarn. I can't say how relived I was. For the next fifteen minutes we clung to each other, until the tide took us back in to the shore a mile or so past the top end of the village.

'Shit, man. That's a bad fucking rip. You don't want to see two of those.' We walked back down the beach to retrieve our things. Lying in the sand among my possessions was the tiny piece of coloured thread.

I had a trusty little radio that kept me in touch with the outside world, supplying me with Radio Four and the World Service and music. One day, on returning from the sea, I found it missing. This upset Raja more than it did me – he felt in some way responsible. 'Come, come,' he said. 'We must go to the old lady.'

The old lizard lady sat me down outside her hut and brought out her pot of fire. She sat in front of me and burned incense and assorted dried leaves. A small crowd gathered to watch. After about half an hour she told me to go home and wait for my radio. The crowd dispersed, and we made our way back to the Coral Sands. On the verandah was my radio in its usual place. Raja smiled broadly, his faith in the old lady's magical powers reaffirmed. Siri, a more practical man, later explained with a sly chuckle, 'The old lady can cast terrible spells. When word reached the thief's ears that she was putting a spell on whoever stole your radio, the culprit couldn't put it back fast enough. Who needs the police when we have superstition and wisdom?'

Kataragama was a nearby holy city sacred to many different creeds. Every seven years a festival at this temple attracts pilgrims from as far away as the Himalayas. A sudden influx of pilgrim traffic through our village alerted me to the impending festival. Incredible fakirs walked through the village en route to Kataragama, naked men covered in ash and symbolic marks, their flesh often speared through with darts and arrows. Some were so dedicated they would walk in shoes made of nails. As the festival approached, the outskirts of the village and adjacent beach became a makeshift stopover for the pilgrims. They would camp there before moving on. Where there are pilgrims there are traders, soothsayers, healers, hustlers, con men, and of course holy men.

One night Raja Singha came to me and asked to show me a very holy man. We walked a mile or so along the beach to a campfire, where a crowd had gathered. The object of their attention was a wiry naked old man. He sat in meditation while his *chella*, a small boy of about seven, administered to his needs and religiously collected alms for his master. Over the fire, hanging from a makeshift A-frame was a cauldron of water. The crowd was waiting for the cauldron of water to boil. With great show, the master dipped a long bundle of leaves into the cauldron and began stirring the contents, which the crowd took it in turns to examine. More wood was thrown on the fire and, lo, the cauldron bubbled furiously. A cry went out to announce that the water was boiling, and many people rushed to

168

Above A desperate James Bond (George Lazenby) forces me to give him a light on board *The Hedonist* in Tangiers, 1970. (*Patrick Lichfield*)

Right Mim and Virginia Parker on a photo-shoot in Tan-Tan, Morocco, 1971. (*Bernard Mignon*)

Below Mim and Putzy on a boat off Praslin Island in the Seychelles, 1971.

Above Mim in the Gazell d'Or garden in Taroudannt, Morocco, 1971. (*CVO*)

Left Putzy with her soul-sister, the Sphinx, Cairo 1973. (*MS*)

Below Shadowfax on the beach in Essa-ouira, Morocco, driving past the ruins of the palace of Mogador, 1974. (*CVO*)

Above A meeting of the G'naoua, Tangiers, 1973. (*The G'naoua*)

Right Reebop Kwaku Baah and the G'naoua in the Marchand House, Tangiers, 1975. *Left to right*, Mohammad Zain, his drummer, Reebop, Mohammad and Abdelkadar. (*Alan Hirsh*)

Below Shadowfax, gravely injured in a Sierra Nevada valley outside Granada, Spain, 1976. (*Dieter Steinert*)

The direct-to-disc recording of the
Warsaw Pakt's *Needle Time* at Trident
Studios, Soho, 1977. *Left to right*, Mim,
centre, John Porter, with Andy Colquhoun
of The Pakt, Hutch, and the Trident staff.

Mim and Marianne Faithfull on the steps
of Cheyne Walk before leaving for
Saturday Night Live in New York, 1977.

Left Denny Cordell, hit-maker and man o
the turf, Carlow, 1987.

the spectacle. The naked master grabbed the rim of the steaming cauldron with both hands, took a deep breath, then plunged his head into the boiling water and held it there for a long time. The crowd remained deathly silent, waiting in anticipation, and gave a mighty gasp as the master, unharmed, pulled his head from the boiling vessel, calmly rewrapped himself in his dottie, and sat back down and went into a trance.

People crept quite close to the fakir to examine his shaven head. There was not a sign of a blister or any kind of injury. The little *chella* ran around furiously with his bowl, collecting more rupees before the crowd dispersed. Raja was very impressed with this trick. He had seen many fakirs, both false and real. He was not easily fooled. Back at the Coral Sands, Siri asked me smilingly if I had enjoyed the show.

'A real magician,' I said.

'Oh no! Mim,' said Siri, nodding his head. 'He is just a clever con man. He used to do conjuring tricks, but now since the Japanese have opened the fish factory in Gale he has found this new trick.'

I was curious. The water in the cauldron had looked horribly hot to me.

Siri chuckled. 'You know when he stirred the leaves into the water?'

'Yes.'

'Well, he hides a lump of what they call cardice, CO_2, bought from the fish factory, in the bundle of twigs. When he stirs the cauldron he drops the CO_2 into the water to make it look like it's boiling. A good trick, eh?'

I had to agree. 'Siri, you don't believe in magic?'

'Of course I do,' he said.

By this time my experiments with LSD and meditation had combined. I was in the perfect place to try to understand the principles of transcendental meditation, and with the weekly

169

and sometimes daily visits to the abbot I was making progress. It didn't matter whether my experiences were drug- or trance-induced; to me they were very real. I was developing the ability to step into separate realties. There were some large rocks just offshore from Hikkaduwa with the remains of a ruined temple on one; I would swim out to these rocks with my paraphernalia wrapped in plastic. My main piece of meditation equipment had been made for me by Michael Wilson during one of his stays in the holy city of Kataragama. It was a highly polished, stainless-steel caduceus which balanced perfectly when spun in the hand, reflecting light from any available source. This had the effect of drawing a light circle for every light source available. During a full moon or starlit night, the endless circles contained a full spectrum of colours. It was a very hypnotic wand. I made huge psychedelic flights up into the monsoon clouds and beyond, soaring to unimaginable heights, in total control, feeling the wind, twisting and turning like a swallow.

One evening I swam out to the ruin – my favourite launch-pad for transcendental flying – with the specific intention of contacting Putzy. She was thousands of miles away in St Moritz. After a tab of Owsley acid, my proposed flight did not seem so daunting. I climbed onto the rocks, unwrapped my wand, my chillum and other necessities from their waterproofing, and began my ceremony. Far out on the horizon the large orange fireball was setting, quivering as it touched the sea. I loved this moment when the sun changed from an orb into a mosque-like shape with a definite point. A monsoon was brewing, and the clouds and sky were closing in.

As I sat on my rock, allowing the acid to warm me and focusing on the point of the sun, I began to spin my wand faster and faster until it appeared to be whipping up the clouds like candy floss. In this way I collected the clouds as one would a spider's web with a feather duster, depositing them back into the sea. Now I could get down to the serious business of

170

flying. I made a few preliminary passes over the beach to get my bearings, dipping and diving, at one with the air and the wind. I remembered that the purpose of my mission was to visit Putzy, so I soared up into the heart of the monsoon, travelling through the turbulence like an arrow, until I swooped down from a great height over the Alps and found familiar ground, the peaks of St Moritz.

Then it all went wrong. There I was, hovering outside Putzy's mountain-top chalet. I could see lights and tried to get in but I couldn't, and as I felt my strength draining I had to turn back. Sometime later I awoke on my rock as if from a dream. The sky had cleared and a tinge of dawn was creeping over the ocean as I wrapped up my things, lowered myself into the sea and swam back to my house. Raja Singha was squatting on the verandah where he had been watching my meditations. He saw me wade ashore before slipping off to bring me a towel, a joint, and a pot of his best tea. Before I retired to bed I wrote a letter to Putzy, describing how I had flown through the storm, found the Alps, and her house, and tapped on windows and doors to no avail before turning for home. I gave the letter to Raja to post before I crashed out.

A few days later I received a letter from her.

Dear Mim,
What are you up to? The most extraordinary thing happened the other night. As you know I have become rather friendly with Michael (he of the crashing cars) and on Tuesday night I asked him to stay with me. He had just undressed and climbed into bed when he jumped out again like a crazy man, claiming that you had flown through the window and sat on him. I'll come to Sri Lanka in the next weeks to explain my feelings for him. I hope you are well.
All my love, Putzy.

171

I was surprised, of course, about the coincidence, but more surprised about my darling little Putzy and the handsome, degenerate Michael. I was deeply in love with her, and this guy was bad news. I knew he was not in love with Putzy.

The day came for me to go into Colombo to meet her plane. We were so pleased to see each other. It had been four months since her last visit. We did not go straight back to Hikkaduwa but took a little tour to Kandy and Polonnaruwa. Putzy was very forthright and told me exactly what was happening to her. She explained that she had fallen for Michael. I was choked but had to admit I had been quite selfish in wanting to stay in Sri Lanka over the past year. How could I have allowed her to be so exposed to my rival's advances?

Chapter Twenty-six

I had recently received a letter from my Cousin Ronnie enclosing the key to *Shadowfax* and explaining he'd had a magical tour of Morocco, experiencing the wonderful freedom of the open road. Everything had been going well until he'd damaged the old Land-Rover so badly in the desert outside La'youn that he could not fix it. He had walked for miles, carrying what he could, and eventually traded a camera to a truck-driver in return for a tow into La'youn. But by the time he had returned to *Shadowfax* it had been stripped by Bedouins who took anything saleable. Ronnie was upset by this but, to his credit, persevered and got the truck into a military base where he left it, telling them that I would come to get it sometime in the future.

Putzy and I stayed in Hikkaduwa for a few more days. I bade a sad farewell to the friends I had made there and she helped me pack my few things. She and I agreed we would never really be apart. While our physical relationship was over, we would take our friendship into another realm.

We flew to Cairo. It was the end of May 1973. I had in my notebook the co-ordinates of the best place to experience a total eclipse in the Sahara. This was due to take place on 29 June, close to where my faithful *Shadowfax* now languished.

On 1 June Putzy and I arrived in Cairo. I wanted to tune the wand that Michael Wilson had made for me with the energy of the Great Pyramid. We ventured out to the deserted pyramid site from the village of Meena late that night. A bribe got the gate-keeper to open the iron gate that sealed the pyramid entrance, and Putzy and I entered. I had dropped some acid to help magnify the experience. We lit a candle and started to mount the chicken-board steps that led up to the various chambers.

During the day the corridors were illuminated with neon that hummed as it generated light, but when the tomb was empty and the lights out, the faint but audible hum remained in the stones. We made our way to the Queen's Chamber. Currents of air of differing temperatures wafted over us. The vast black sarcophagus of the queen lay empty and slightly damaged. We sat in the centre of the chamber as I spun my wand probing for a contact with the past, the acid full-on by now. I was flying. We blew the candle out and held hands, plunged into primeval darkness, letting those who wished to visit us come. Eventually we made our way down the steep steps to the gate and stepped out into the Sahara sand where Yala, who had organized our nocturnal visit, was waiting with horses. A thin Arabian moon hung beautifully in the sky as the three of us rode off into the desert in search of the shack of Mohammad the Hashisheen.

Yala was an extraordinary person who had hustled tourists since he could walk and talk. He hung back from the scrum and watched as his rivals tried to rent us their horses. I caught his eye and he beckoned to me. Putzy and I strolled over to him, followed by the bartering crowd of horse dealers. Yala shooed away the opposition with a wave of his hand and an Egyptian curse.

'My friends, you want a romantic ride in the desert? You want to be Mark Antony and Cleopatra? Come, follow me.'

We followed Yala into the village and the narrow streets of Meena. During the walk he explained that he had hung out

174

every day of his life at the base of the Great Pyramid, teaching himself English, French, Italian and German.

'When I was very young, I realized that all of the greatest people in the world want to visit the pyramid, and that most of them eventually will. So every day I wait and watch.'

Yala swaggered, the breeze billowing his flowing white robe, as we penetrated ever narrower streets. The stucco walls seemed to grow up out of the sand. From out of the blinding sunshine he led us into the cool shadows of a nondescript doorway, which he opened with a large key. We found ourselves in a beautiful, shady courtyard oasis. Roses and other flowers grew neatly in colourful pots. Yala offered us cushions in a shady spot by the fountain.

'Hashish?' said Yala, producing a small pipe.

'I thought you'd never ask,' I replied.

We settled down to talk and smoke, and a girl came over with the tea tray. Although he had never been to school, Yala was one of the most articulate men I have ever met.

With the wind in our hair and the crescent moon floating above the three pyramids, we galloped after our escort, following him into the desert night. Eventually, we stopped at the tent of the hashisheen, tucked into some medium-sized dunes. We tethered the horses and went inside, where we were greeted by a wizened old nomad tending a small fire of charcoal, next to which was a battered water-pipe. We had spent hours alone in the dark, inside the Queen's Chamber of the Great Pyramid, ridden across the moonlit Nile valley on Arabian horses, and were now confronted by the daunting pipe of a very serious hashisheen.

This was hippie heaven.

Putzy and I said goodbye at Cairo airport. She flew out to Zürich and I to Las Palmas in the Canaries. I watched her plane streak into the desert sky.

The route from Cairo to Mauritania overland would have taken me months, and I wanted to be there for 29 June 1973, the date of the total eclipse. From Las Palmas I took a boat to La'youn on the west coast of the Spanish Sahara. I headed for the gas station on the town's outskirts where I had been told I might find a camion ride into Mauritania, took directions to the army base and found my way there.

After a bit of searching and bureaucratic hustle I found *Shadowfax*. The old truck was on blocks, but it looked okay. There was a corrugated hut inside the compound and I went and introduced myself. After much thumbing through a ledger and comparing my name on the logbook with the registration number of the truck, the chief admitted that the truck was indeed mine and that I could take it away — after the small matter of storage costs was settled. Frankly, I did not mind, I was so pleased to be reunited.

We walked over to the dead truck, I touched it, and with some apprehension put the key in and turned it one click to prime the diesel, then again to full ignition. To my amazement the old engine tried to turn over, spoke twice and then died. I asked about the wheels and was pointed to the stucco and adobe walls of the nearby village. I thanked the chief and told him I would be back.

The first building in the village was a sort of *tienda* that sold everything from Coca-Cola to dates, diesel and bread. On top of six diesel barrels were my six wheels, each acting as a date bowl. After much negotiation in Spanish, French and pissed-off English, I bought my wheels and soon they were being rolled to the compound by a small gang of young kids.

It was unbelievable: there was *Shadowfax*, its wheels back on. A quick inspection revealed that most of the seats were missing, the manifold was broken, snapped off at the block, the interior of the truck had been trashed and my speakers levered open, though the eight-track tape player was still bolted to the roof of the cab. The poor old thing was a sorry sight. We pushed the truck out of the compound to a yard that called itself a garage, whose chief mechanic appeared to be no more than twelve years old, a cheeky urchin in dungarees with spanners hanging from bits of torn pockets.

It was now the 11th. The repair of *Shadowfax* became the main topic of conversation in the village. It helped take my mind off Putzy as the repairs became a communal effort. Things that had been missing started to reappear. The seats came back, and the wife of the *tienda* owner made me new curtains from black and white Mauritanian cloth. We stripped the engine and waited for a manifold from Casablanca. On the 23rd I was able to take *Shadowfax* on a test run around the village to cheers of the kids, my little mechanic triumphantly riding shotgun on the bonnet. I loaded up with fruit, bread and water, paid my bills, and waved goodbye to my friends as I set off to meet the eclipsing sun.

I flew across the Sahara to the sound of Bobby Keys and the Rolling Stones from the solitary cassette that had remained in the wreck.

I was determined to find the best vantage point in Mauritania. As evening fell I saw lights in the distance and headed for them. They led me to the camp of an eclipse observers' convention, who invited me to join them for dinner. They had all manner of equipment: telescopes of every shape and size, scientific equipment to measure ultraviolet and infrared light rays. The next morning I checked my compass reading and took off. I found a valley of giant dunes with pristine knife-cut edges that swept away to the south with a magnificent view of the Sahara. I parked the truck, made camp, dropped a couple of windowpanes and sat naked in the sand except for three pairs of cheap shades I had sellotaped together, to await the meeting of the moon and sun. I felt overwhelmed by the privilege of having so much of planet earth to myself, the only seat in an incredible cosmic theatre, waiting to witness a movie directed and staged by the gods themselves. Out of all my drug experiences, this and the controlled illusion of flying were the closest I came to truly experiencing a totally separate reality.

I spent the rest of the day meditating. The sky gave no indication of what was about to happen. Then the moon took its first minuscule bite out of the sun, imperceptibly drifting across its face, the sky darkening all the while, until the covering of the sun was absolute. The dunes that surrounded me were made of billions of balanced crystal grains of sand, and as I watched in the strange eclipse light, they seemed to collapse at their peaks and sink into themselves all the way to the horizon. Suddenly an incredible streak of light swept across the sky, that first chink of sunlight breaking from behind the dark moon. I was back in the Sahara alone and uplifted beyond words. Eventually I slept.

A sound entered my dreams, so persistently that it woke me from my deep acid sleep. I can't describe the sound other than that it was animal. It was still dark outside and I was in the middle of the Sahara. I shivered and pulled the curtains, instinctively checking the doors. In the morning I looked out and saw my own footprints accompanied by paw prints in the otherwise pristine sand. I followed them around the dunes but found nothing as the prints doubled up on each other. I packed up camp and headed for Morocco.

I drove all day with the Spanish Sahara unfolding before me. That night I heard the same noise. It was scary. In the morning the same paw prints were all about my camp, but I could find no beginning or end to the trail. I continued my journey, entering Morocco through the spectacular Vallée du Dra. I drove non-stop up to Tangiers.

It had been a long, obsessive drive. It was unlike me to cross Morocco without stopping at any of my favourite places. It was my intention to stay at the Atlas Hotel, but I caught a glimpse of myself in the windscreen. My Sri Lankan complexion had been compounded by African sun. I was black, my hair long and decorated with silver beads. I was wearing a blue robe, which needed a wash, and I was covered in desert dust.

Instead of driving into town, I skipped around the coast road to Cap Spartel and parked on the clifftop. I walked down to the sea with my wand and flute, undressed and made a neat pile of my possessions. The sea was warm and fresh after days of desert. I floated on my back looking at the Moroccan sky and listening to the lapping of the waves.

Then I heard it. It was the sound of the gimbri drifting faintly over the calm water to my ears. I had to concentrate to hear it, but yes, it was definitely a gimbri, the instrument of the G'naoua that I had been seeking for so long. I swam to the shore and crossed the sand in the direction of the music. As I walked the music grew less faint. I could now hear it clearly, and there were other instruments – drums, castanets, chanting. It was quite a dark night, but not too dark to see shapes. In a cove the silhouette of a large tent appeared. On the sand were the embers of a fire, still aglow, but resting. The beach was alive with the steady rhythm of the music. The music that I had been searching for since my arrival in Morocco, the magic music of the G'naoua, was coming from the tent.

Chapter Twenty-seven

Spinning my wand in time to the music, I approached the tent. I lifted the flap and looked in at some thirty people. Some of them were standing, some sitting, and others lying on the floor covered in coloured cloth sheets. At one end the musicians sat on a woven rug: a gimbri player, a drummer, a bindir player, and a fourth playing the castanets. The interior of the tent was bathed in a mysterious blue haze. The rhythm that was playing as I entered was, as I discovered later, from Sidi Mussa. Some of the gathering were in a deep trance and danced, pounding their bare feet on the sand floor. A woman with a basketful of coloured scarves covered those who occasionally fainted.

The musician playing the gimbri was Sidi Abdelkader. He was wearing the robe of the master-musician. Whether I fainted from exhaustion from the long drive or the hypnotic effect of the music I don't know, but I awoke lying on a rug and covered with a soft *hiak* blanket. A fire crackled on the beach and children played around me in the sand. An American who had lived in Tangiers for several years brought me some coffee. He asked if I knew what had happened to me. I told him that I had been following the music for a couple of years and that last night was the first time I had actually heard it face to face. He said he knew this, that Sidi Abdelkader had told him about me and my search. 'Welcome to the music, my friend,' the big man said, as he offered his hand.

He introduced me to the others, some of whom I recognized

from the Petit Socco. Everyone was terribly nice to me. I spent the day on the beach at Cap Spartel. The tent had been pitched at the spot where the Atlantic meets the Mediterranean, the ancient ceremonial place where the pillars of Hercules once stood. The music I had heard was in honour of Sidi Mussa — Poseidon to the Greeks, or Neptune to the Romans. They all have dominion over water, and an association with the colour blue. I explained to my new friends that I had been searching for the master of the gimbri. I had to learn for myself if this was the root music of rock and roll. I explained that it was just something that Brian and I had decided to do.

Centuries ago, slavers combed the west coast of Africa, and the black warriors of Dahomey stole whole populations of villages. The shamen as well as ordinary folk were chained and taken away. Imagine tending a beautiful garden in a coastal village in west Africa, the domestic animals and children blissfully playing in the sunshine, the chieftain in his perfectly constructed *kraal*, the young hunters returning with their game, the women weaving on looms hung beneath the shade of acacia trees. Then at night a devilish army raids the village and captures all living souls, marching them through the night to the beach and into the holds of the dark ships. A musician shaman would sing, and soon all the captives in the dark holds would be chanting, the sea rough, the slaves frightened. The survivors would have been brought out into daylight on the shores of America, in shock but saved by the shaman's magic; brought back from a visit to hell by a musical instrument made from a tortoise-shell, a piece of wood and some goat gut. Soon the slaves had their music back and their religion. The leap from tortoise-shell gimbri to banjo to guitar was natural. Soon shamen like Uncle Remus, Leadbelly, Robert Johnson and Chuck Berry were playing these instruments as master-musicians, and rock and roll was born.

*   *   *

181

The next day I parked *Shadowfax* outside the Café Hiafa ('café of the cats') while I went on a house hunt. The house next door to the café itself was for rent, a beautiful house just outside the kasbah. It had a main room with French windows that opened onto the sea. It was built on the clifftop and was perfect for my needs. I retired to the café for a *sebsis* and a pot of tea. The Café Hiafa was carved out of the living rock. Twenty or so small terraces had been cut from the cliff, joined to each other by pathways and flowerbeds. Each small terrace had rugs and a sublime view over the straits of Gibraltar. The other feature of the Café Hiafa was its cats. The owner adopted any stray in the area, feeding them every day at five o'clock. It was wonderful to watch the relationship he had with them. I sat on a terrace and smoked a few bowls, then strolled back to *Shadowfax*.

My heart sank as I noticed that the driver's door was open. I climbed in. Everything seemed in order: the gris-gris and Sahara charms that decorated the cab dangled in the breeze, the seat covers were in place – and a cash stash under them. But my safe-box was on the floor, and it was open. I examined the box and there was my passport and my traveller's cheques.

Then I heard a very loud, familiar, frightening noise, the same as I'd heard during those nights in Mauritania. It made the hair on the back of my neck stand up. I sat still and listened. This time it had something recognizable in it. I should have known it earlier. It was a distressed cat, and the noise was coming from under my seat. I climbed out, looked under the truck and saw nothing unusual, but I heard the sound again. I found my torch and crawled under, exploring every crevice with a beam of light until two glowing orbs reflected back at me. I made an attempt to get close to whatever it was, but it backed into the recesses of the axle casing. After several failed attempts I tried a new ploy: I put a saucer of milk under the truck. Fifteen minutes later a horrible creature jumped down from its hiding place, a matted little devil with a bloated belly and skinny legs, its only redeeming feature a pair of beautiful eyes. I watched it guzzle the milk and then made a flying dive at it with a towel and caught the thing. Naturally it went berserk, drawing blood as it bit and scratched. I could see fleas and lice crawling all over the creature's head, covered in axle-grease and sand. I made a makeshift bag from an old towel and left the little monster in it while I filled a bucket.

By this time I had attracted a crowd of inquisitive kids. I mixed half a bottle of shampoo into the bucket, then grabbed the thing by the scruff, dipped it in and scrubbed. Ten minutes and several scratches later I wrapped a grey-and-white, feral, desert tabby in a dry towel and threw the writhing bundle into the truck. The children and I spent the next half hour walking around the truck peering through the windows to watch its progress. He went mad at first and ran around and around and around, diving over the seats looking for a means of escape. But slowly he settled down. He was eventually tamed and named Abdullah Sphinx, becoming the best-known cat in Morocco, and my very best friend.

I deduced that Abdullah had ventured out for a bit of a lizard hunt during the eclipse and found me. How he managed to survive the journey, crouching in the chassis for the best part of a thousand miles, I will never know. Whoever was trying to break into *Shadowfax* saw the gris-gris and other bits of Sahara magic decorating the cab, and then must have heard the same blood-curdling scream that had frightened me – quite enough to send any *djinn*-fearing thief scuttling off.

I moved into the Hiafa house. Over the next few months I was introduced to the G'naoua musicians and started to befriend their friends. My house became their house; people would come and go and talk and play music. One night I was sitting by the fireplace in the main room, smoking a water-pipe and watching the seagulls gliding in the updraught outside, when

183

Abdelkader came by with several musicians, one of whom had a cockerel under his arm. The cockerel was dispatched and its blood drained into a bowl and studied. Some sort of divination was going down. When they had finished, music was played to accompany the sunset over Spain on the far horizon. Eventually the party broke up and everyone left. Alone in the house, I made myself comfortable, put some logs on the fire, had a nice smoke and started to play my flute. It was one that I had made myself from a lovely piece of root bamboo, its design based on the Peruvian flute. I had taken it everywhere with me, and I could play it quite well if inconsistently.

This time the flute came to life without any real coaxing. I was wailing away, my eyes closed, lost in a marijuana groove. Suddenly I became aware that I was playing stuff that was out of my league. The sounds that I was making now and the control that I had over them was a new experience. The more I played the better the music became. It was a fantastical experience to be playing brilliant music for the first time in my life. But I could not stop playing. The room took on a strange atmosphere; the breeze from the sea whipped up the curtains in the open window, the fire jumped and spat sparks into the copper canopy that hung from the ceiling. It was alarming as I realized I was not the one playing.

I tried to put the flute down and was torn between the part of me that wanted to continue to play the music at all costs, and the part of me that wanted to stop. I felt I was being possessed by a music-making *djinn*. Had the G'naoua musicians conjured it up as some kind of initiation?

The room became wilder and wilder as I sat transfixed in my chair, my fingers fluttering over the flute, the sounds wailing into the breeze that appeared to be getting stronger. The windows were banging, and I was powerless to stop my mystical, musical frenzy. I recalled comments by the abbot in Hikkaduwa: When the dragon comes you must give him a saucer of milk. This thought obsessed me for a while, until I struggled out of the chair and fought my way to the kitchen still playing the flute. I felt like I was walking through treacle. With a huge effort I put down the instrument but the music seemed to continue. I grabbed a bottle of milk from the refrigerator, poured some into a saucer, and put it by the fire.

The breeze dropped, the music stopped, and the whole house calmed down. Abdullah Sphinx climbed onto my shoulder, smelt the milk in the nearby saucer and was soon purring and lapping away at my offering. It calmed me to watch him.

Suddenly it was daylight and the gulls were again squawking outside the windows as they hovered in the updraught from the cliffs. A knock at the door startled me. It was the musicians armed with fresh, sweet-smelling breakfast bread, Zibda, grapes and goat's cheese. 'Good morning, Mim, have you had a good night?'

It was decided that I should record the G'naoua music. I was thrilled, but I needed money to do it. I was owed some cash by a jewellery dealer in Munich, so *Shadowfax* made good time crossing Spain and France and on to Germany. I arrived in Munich at night and went directly to the dealer's shop, which was closed, so I cruised around settling for a parking space in the English Garden, a small park in the centre of town.

Abdullah was by now an accomplished trucker. He would travel on my shoulder like a fur collar, his head up against the speaker behind the driver's seat. When I stopped he would jump out, do his business and go hunting. He behaved more like a dog than a cat. Wherever he was, if he heard me start the truck he would come scampering back, jump in and be ready to travel. He would also bring me presents like dead bats, mice, worms and frogs. I let him out in the English Garden and settled down for a good sleep.

The park was at that time a hippie paradise. Clusters of

guitar-players sat around smoking and grooving. The girls of Munich seemed more beautiful than their counterparts in the rest of Europe. And the park was the best place in town to score dope. I had just dozed off when I heard a thumping on the door, and then in a Texan drawl, 'Hey, Mim, are you in there? It's Bobby, man, Bobby Keys.'

'Come on in, what are you doing in the park?'

'Trying to score, man.'

I had not seen Bobby since the summer of *Goat's Head Soup*. He had recognized *Shadowfax*.

'I'm staying at the Hilton with the Stones. We have a concert at the Olympic Stadium tomorrow night. Let's go. Keith would love to see you.'

I gave Bobby a lump of my best Tangiers hash and arranged to visit the Hilton the next day. The place was humming. Bobby had given me the code name for the Stones, and I was soon whooshing up to the penthouse in a high-speed lift. As usual the whole of the top floor was Stones territory, and I saw all the familiar faces of the entourage. I was content to get high and watch the show begin to roll.

From the penthouse windows we could see the Olympic Stadium, scene of the diabolical bomb at the 1972 games. Through binoculars we watched the stadium filling up as the sun went down behind it. Keith was an hour away from a major concert and yet here he was, laid back and looning with his entourage. Bianca was an official Stones woman; Ushi and the other gorgeous creatures in the suite weren't. It was decided that they should travel in *Shadowfax* with me.

Suddenly it was showtime; the last call had been made and we all swept out of the suite and into the lifts, a bunch of stoned vagabonds. The lift stopped at the next floor to let in the rest of the show, the inimitable Billy Preston and Co. They had a completely different look to the Stones. Billy and his gang were superspades, with massive Afros and glitter flares. The lift continued its downward journey, spilling its psychedelic cargo out into a lobby full of hundreds of grey-suited dentists on a convention. The contrast was fantastic. We pressed through to the street where the Stones climbed aboard their bus, and Ushi and her girlfriends climbed into *Shadowfax* with myself and Abdullah.

Blue flashing lights announced our escort – four immaculate Mercedes, full of uniformed German cops. The bus took off, I followed, the lights and sirens flashed and screamed. *Shadowfax* was not exactly a suitable Autobahn vehicle and couldn't travel at more than sixty-five miles an hour, but Keith had the bus slow down so that by the time the procession swooped into the underground tunnel that led to the stage we were all together. The bus stopped on the stage as did *Shadowfax*. There was a scramble to get out of the vehicles as the Stones led by Keith fell from the bus, dressed and ready to rock. The huge crowd gave a mighty roar as Charlie hit his drums, and the Stones were off and running.

To find myself backstage on acid with the Stones just a few days after being tripped out by the G'naoua masters in Tangiers, was for me what the Sufis call *tajali*, the science of coincidence. It was amazing I should run into the Stones so soon after being initiated by the master-musicians that Brian and I had set our hearts on finding. As I stood grooving to the greatest rock and roll band in the world, the spirit of Brian was with me, as it had been throughout my journey.

I left for London, my mission now to record the G'naoua music. I set up base with Philip Harvey in the Portobello Road, and started looking for equipment. I bought a Revox from Peter Frampton, a few microphones, an eight-track mixer and a couple of boxes of quarter-inch tape, and soon I was ready to return.

I was back in Tangiers in November 1973. I moved a

musician called Richard and his wife into a spare room to help me set about making the main room of the Hiafa house into a recording studio. We experimented with the microphone placement, because once the music started, what you heard was what you got – refrigerator hum, fire crackles, kif coughs and all. Over the next few months we learned a great deal about Moroccan music, as well as the customs and way of life inside Tangiers. I had become familiar with the Koran, and this kindled my interest in Sufis. Islamic scholars, writers, poets and painters had always found inspiration, both spiritual and physical, in Tangiers. It was a revelation to be living there, surrounded by the music, philosophy, history and culture of that ancient city. The more absorbed I became the more secrets the city yielded. Many friends helped me to understand the culture, and the cultures within the culture, among them Paul Bowles (so integrated with Tangiers life that he was almost Moroccan), Brion Gysin and Claudio Bravo the painter. Possession by demons, healing by holy men and women, and exorcism, were all considered normal in Tangiers. Music was an expression of these beliefs.

Fundamental laws apply to all of the secret sects of musicians in Africa. Any sect is only as powerful as its shaman. Masters still teach pupils the sacred arts, of trance, music, colour and rhythm. The elect needs very special qualities to become a master shaman – the art cannot be placed in an unsuitable vessel. There are people in Africa who can play the birds out of the trees, the devil out of tormented souls, and the illness out of a sick body. Tangiers had its share of such people. And the city protected them.

I wanted to try to organize proper recordings, but I didn't want to take the G'naoua into a studio, which would have spoilt the spontaneity of their music. But I did want to record their music for posterity. I took it for granted that the recordings would be a labour of love. It was unlikely at that time that they

188

were going to have any great commercial value ('world music' had no significant market in the 1970s). But from a cultural, artistic and historical viewpoint, the proposed recordings had great importance.

G'naoua culture was changing fast. Their children were now exposed to radio and cassettes and Western popular culture. A decade earlier the live music of the sect would have been the only music that the children of the G'naoua would have heard. Their music might be lost as a result of these changes.

I had been in the Hiafa house for four months now and felt like a resident of Tangiers. I loved living there. My daily walk to the markets took me through the kasbah where my friends were. I knew the passageways of the city intimately. When I fell down and lay unconscious in one of these alleyways late one night, I was recognized and helped by friends of the G'naoua, who took me to the Italian Hospital where chronic hepatitis A was diagnosed. The nuns at the Italian hospital were remarkable and totally dedicated. I opened my eyes to see several diminutive figures looking at me, their white winged headdresses giving the impression of angels' wings. For six weeks I had intravenous drips and a diet of steamed fish and dry bread, supplemented by special soups brought by members of the G'naoua. The treatment worked and eventually I was well enough to leave the hospital. I owed my life to them and was told afterwards that I nearly died during the first couple of weeks in hospital.

I rested and spent time in Marbella with Gavin, then drove through France to St-Tropez where I stopped off at the Tower of the Sails to see Putzy. The house was full of Michael's friends and though Putzy was pleased to see me and hear the music, she was in love with Michael. I stayed for a few days but this turned out to be too painful for me. It became obvious that Michael was two-timing her. He had imported a girlfriend from

Munich. I couldn't tell Putzy what I knew, as I'd sound jealous. I drove to Ibiza and rented a small house in Santa Gertrudes, where I worked on the G'naoua tapes, supporting myself with jewellery sales.

At the end of 1974, I felt strong enough to return to London and spend Christmas with my mother in Forest Hill. I began to look for release possibilities for my G'naoua recordings, but the commercial record companies were not interested in world music. It would take another decade before they learned how to market it under the heading of Ambient Music.

Inspired by the adventures of *Shadowfax*, my friend Michael Pearson was toying with the idea of crossing Asia. He would need a vehicle big enough to accommodate six people comfortably, capable of all-terrain travel, and able to move fast on metalled roads. The only people I knew who could build such a truck were in Los Angeles.

Chapter Twenty-eight

I had some good friends in Hollywood. Jacqueline Bisset was living in one of the canyons; Sally Savalas was with Telly and her children; Nicholas and Nicolette in Bel Air; Stewart Levine had a house on the beach in Malibu, as did Denny Cordell. Hollywood is hell on earth. By train, by plane, by bus, by car, they come in search of the dream. Most find bitter disappointment, and if lucky they will leave the city of dreams with only their pride and self-respect damaged.

There are two intertwined industries in Hollywood, music and film, both controlled by a handful of men. These dragons sit at the top and need to be fed on their special diet of juicy talent, their tentacles running through the city, through producers, agents, casting directors, actors, writers, photographers, studio personnel, desk clerks, hustlers, pimps – on and on to the outskirts of town, constantly licking, seeking a likely morsel. A fraction will get to the hall of fame, the rest are consumed and used. There will never be a shortage of fodder for the dream machine.

I started work on Michael's supertruck in a garage in Anaheim. Michael was commuting, so we rented a house. Just before I left London, someone had given me a gram or two of a new drug called PMA. I didn't have a clue what it was but I suspected that it was a cross between Angel Dust and sulphate. The effect of this substance was spectacular. I had tried it out

191

in the company of some friends in London, including Timothy Leary's wife Joanna.

Shortly after this, Joanna left for Los Angeles to see her husband Timothy who was in jail for drug offences. Progress on the truck was going well, so I went back to London for a few days. On my return to L.A. Joanna was waiting at the airport with a limo. She offered me a ride into town – I accepted and walked to the car. She introduced me to the driver and a guy in a tartan jacket and shades.

During the drive to Sunset Boulevard one of the guys in the car asked me if I had any PMA. I was more than a bit surprised by this and asked to be dropped at the Chateau Marmont. Joanna invited me to have a drink at her hotel and before I could object the stretch pulled into the Sunset Hyatt House. I found myself in her suite with a number of other people behaving very hyperactively. One of the guys repeated his question about the PMA.

I began to feel uncomfortable. 'How much of this stuff can your man make?' someone asked, referring to the amateur Portobello road scientist who had given me the smidgen of PMA in the first place.

'I don't know,' I replied. The cooler of the two guys asked to see the PMA. I produced my tiny stash. The guy looked at it, tasted it, sniffed a tiny dot of it and asked if he could get it analysed. 'Sure,' I said, as interested as him to know what it was.

'If this is as good as its rep, I would order half a ton.'

This was too heavy for me, and I made a move to leave. 'I really must go, keep that and enjoy yourselves.'

In the meantime Joanna and tartan jacket were discussing fur coats. It could have been a scene from a Tarantino movie. The cool guy gave me his card and asked me to call him after I had spoken to my man. He said he would call me if he liked what was in the packet. I hustled away and jumped a cab to

192

the house in Vista Crest, relieved to be out of there. I sat by the pool with a drink, worried that they thought I was a big-time dope-dealer.

I tried to forget the incident but it kept coming back to me. I figured she had got herself into some sort of weird drug action and, as Timothy Leary's wife, was perhaps moving in mega-drug circles. Over the next few days I had a lot to do, driving back and forth to Anaheim to inspect progress on Michael's truck. He was due to arrive any day now. I took a stroll for a bit of breakfast at the Source on Sunset and picked up a copy of the *Los Angeles Times*. The headline leapt off the page: 'Mrs Leary Busts Timothy's Lawyer.' There were pictures of Joanna and Timothy in jail and one of Timothy's lawyers. It said that the lawyer in question had been bringing drugs into prison for him. The article implied that Joanna had cut a deal with the Federal Bureau of Narcotics whereby in return for lenient treatment of Timothy she would give up the names of several big-time drug dealers.

I tried to eat my breakfast and stave off my paranoia. Who were the people in Joanna's hotel suite? Were they drug manufacturers, or were they the FBI? Either way I was involved. There was only one thing to do. I was just a slightly weird English visitor to L.A., with no connection to these people, so I decided to front it out. If Joanna's friends were the FBI, I was probably on film from hidden cameras in the Hyatt House. I needed to clear things up. I would just tell the truth. I dialled the number on the card I had been given in the Hyatt House. It had the name Joe scrawled on it.

'Can I speak to Joe, please?'

'Hold on, sir. Who shall I say is calling?'

'Tell him it's Mim, Joanna's friend.'

After a lot of clicking Joe came to the phone. 'Hello,' I said. 'Have you seen the *L.A. Times*? I think we'd better talk.'

I arranged to meet on the corner of Vista Crest and Mulholland

Drive. I had been instructed to walk along Mulholland. After a couple of hundred yards a black limousine pulled up beside me, the door opened – just like in the movies – and I got in. There were all the same guys from the airport.

The cool guy, the one who took my sample of PMA, said, 'You have something to say to us?'

I was scared. 'Look, Joe, I don't know if you are the good guys or the bad guys. I have just read the *L.A. Times* and the exposé on Joanna.' I produced the newspaper. 'The truth of the matter is that I am not a drug dealer, I'm just an English traveller having a good time in L.A. I'm sorry to disappoint you.'

There was a pregnant pause.

'So who are you?' I asked.

Joe answered. 'You don't want to know. Now listen to me. I am going to stop the car, and you are going to get out, and if you want to stay in L.A. keep your nose clean.'

The car pulled over, the door opened, and I climbed out. Joe stopped me. 'Hey, Mim. If I were you I wouldn't do any more of that PMA shit, it's poison.'

I walked home feeling slightly relieved.

Michael and I decided to leave town for a few days so we drove down to Palm Springs with Tom Keys and a couple of friends, stopping over at Johnny von Newman's, whom I hadn't seen since St-Tropez. He lived in a crazy desert house, had a dozen bikes, and a yardful of fun vehicles. Michael took off in the camper to explore Joshua Tree National Park, leaving Tom and me to drop the mescaline we had saved for the trip.

We went to a place called Ted's Mountain; the mescaline soon had us under its hallucinogenic spell. I set off cross-country and came to a mountain. Fearless, and very stoned, I started to climb. Scrambling over a boulder, I trod on a beautiful little cactus. My foot then slipped and I crashed backwards and slithered down the mountain. With a thump and a cloud of dust, I landed at the foot of a strange rock formation, like an abstract rock statue of Ganesha, the Indian elephant god. I stared up at the rock. The rock stared back.

'Clumsy fool,' it said. I thought it referred to my fall. 'No, the cactus, you fool. You killed a young life. You can't walk here unless you can see.'

I lay there hurting slightly until I apologized and asked permission to proceed.

'You are capable but forgetful, proceed with care.'

I climbed to my feet and returned to the rock face, limping slightly. This time I made better progress and made my way to the summit. It was a real pleasure to be on this small mountain, the view of the desert diminishing as I got higher. At the top, I could see Joshua trees in all directions far below me. Up here, tilting slightly in the wind, was a weathered old rocking chair. The grain in the wood stood proud, the softer parts eaten by years of wind. The temptation to sit in it was immense. But in my condition I had to be careful. I shouted down the mountain to my mentor, the Ganesha rock, 'Can I sit in the chair?'

'Can you?' the rock answered.

I gave it a try and sat in the chair. A yellow lizard scuttled away.

I settled down, and rocked gently, drinking in a magnificent view of the Californian desert, intense colours vibrating from the rocks in the heat haze. Something out of place caught my eye, a lump of stone that had cracked in the desert night and was upside-down. This disturbed my hallucination. I climbed out of my chair, walked over, picked up the offending chunk and turned it over to its correct position in nature. A small rag bundle the size of a golf-ball lay under it. The bundle was of weathered calico. I unwrapped it slowly, as if it was the most precious thing on earth. At its centre was a smaller package wrapped in a different cloth. I unwrapped this too, revealing a spoonful of herbs and organic substance. I knew I should smoke

195

it, filled my chillum, and puffed it up. A breeze blew in my face. A hawk flew over with a rustling shadow.

For a moment I wondered how Tom was getting on. Then down in the valley the Joshua trees started to dance and came together to form intricate patterns, like Navajo beadwork. I watched until it became dark, and the vision subsided. I was hungry, thirsty and cold. I had no idea of time. Stars twinkled in the sky and one lone light twinkled in the valley. It was the fire that Michael and his friend Caroline had made. When I got there I saw Tom was squatting in a blanket and grinning like a Cheshire cat.

'Had a good trip?' said Michael.

'Not bad,' said I. 'Is that coffee I smell?'

I discovered later from a native of Joshua Tree that the trees here dance by their very nature. Not like the dance of a willow or an elm in a breeze but in the fashion I had witnessed. When a Joshua tree reaches maturity, a limb will break away like a man letting an outstretched arm fall. It will drop its hand to the ground. This hand takes root and becomes a new Joshua tree. The old one rots away leaving a new tree to continue the perpetual slow-motion cartwheels around the desert. If one has the patience, or a little mescaline, it is not unusual to see the Joshuas dance.

Chapter Twenty-nine

Chris Blackwell had opened an Island Records office in L.A., so naturally I took my G'naoua tapes to him. Blackwell liked the idea enough to send me to Jamaica to discuss it with his compadre Dicko Jobson. In the peace and tranquillity of Strawberry Hill, Dicko and I hatched a plot to go back to Tangiers. Dicko would have been a Barbary pirate in another age. He was always ready for an adventure. I talked him into joining my G'naoua project.

It was now December 1975. I arrived back in London to find that Chris had converted the Basing Street church in Westbourne Grove into the reggae centre of the world. In the six or so years since I had left London, Island Records had become a major record company. Cat Stevens was, of course, a huge-selling act, but Island had also signed a lot of Jamaican artists and was now pumping reggae into the mainstream. It had always been Chris's intention to put Jamaican music onto the world stage, and he and Bob Marley were now doing just that.

Michael Pearson bought a new house, No. 7 The Boltons, one of the most elegant addresses in London. The house had been completely refurbished and decorated to suit Michael's tastes. In the basement was a twenty-seat cinema that converted, with the pull of a lever, into a full-length shooting gallery. The house had a swimming-pool, sunken baths, a massive studio, loads of bedrooms and reception rooms. On the top floor was a tented suite with furniture and hangings that we had found in Morocco.

I had nowhere to live in London until Michael generously offered me a temporary resting place. I had been travelling around the country in *Shadowfax* and saw nothing unusual in moving from tipi communes in Wiltshire and Wales to the luxury of a grand town house. Michael enjoyed his friends' creativity and encouraged it. The artists Willie Fielding and Bones Jones were beneficiaries of his friendship too; both of them produced their best work under his patronage. Willie, Bones and I often found ourselves house-minding under the watchful eye of Spanish Pedro, the diminutive dandy of a butler. Willie's easel was permanently set up in the huge studio. My music equipment filled the Moroccan suite at the top of No. 7.

In autumn 1976 it was time to accept Island's offer to finance my G'naoua project in Tangiers. Dicko came in from Jamaica to join me as co-producer. The word spread that Mim and Dicko were putting together a trip to Tangiers to record a sect of hash-smoking dervishes, so volunteers from Island's big family rushed to join the expedition. The informal approach adopted by Blackwell from the inception of his record company worked brilliantly. All manner of projects were hatched and put together by Chris's main soldiers, managing director Tim Clarke, chief assistant Denise Mills, chief fixer Suzette Newman, and in-house lawyer Tom Hays. The war room at St Peter's Square was the creative hub of the record company. The music factory was out the back, where the rehearsal rooms and basement studio pumped out music twenty-four hours a day: Bob Marley, Traffic, Robert Palmer, Ijaman, Burning Spear, Inner Circle. Any of the Island staff could stroll out the back for a listen to the rehearsals, and if you raided the kitchen you might be lucky enough to get a taste of Lucky Gordon's

198

Jamaican cooking. Downstairs at St Peter's Square was a small but efficient studio where all Island products got the final touch. Chris himself would come in, listen to a mix, comment, change a bass line and make a hit. I loved that dark little room with its mellow lights and huge Neve mixing-desk.

In a corner of this studio were the conga drums of Reebop Kwaku Baah. Reebop was a remarkable musician who had been trained to play drums for the king of his tribe in Nigeria. Somehow he and his drum had made it to London where he spent nights playing in Soho with the legendary Speedy at the All-Nighter, jamming with Graham Bond, and Georgie Fame.

In 1971 Steve Winwood invited Reebop to join Traffic. Jim Capaldi's drums, backed up with Reebop's percussion and the bass of Roscoe, gave Steve the perfect platform for his vocal and keyboard talents. But Traffic split up and Reebop once again became an itinerant musician. If congas were needed by a rock and roll band, Reebop got the call. That is, if they could find him. Reebop had the disconcerting habit of occasionally getting very drunk. This often ignited his considerable temper, creating havoc and resulting in the odd arrest. He was, however, a very sweet guy and a powerful talent, and was therefore always forgiven.

The G'naoua had asked me once to bring a musician back with me, as they were anxious to experience first-hand 'rock and roll'. After much consideration I decided that I wanted to take Reebop and his drums to Tangiers. I reckoned that a confrontation between the Nigerian rock drums of Reebop and the gimbri of Abdelkader could be a potent musical vortex. The rest of the round table agreed. John Porter had been the guitarist and producer of early Roxy Music albums with Brian Ferry. He would also be a great asset to the project. The only problem was how to get Reebop to Tangiers at the appropriate time.

I stayed in London organizing and sent Dicko off to Tangiers to find a suitable house to rent which we could use as our studio. I sent to Munich for a friend of Putzy's called Dieter Steinert, who was a good trucker. We had already travelled together and I knew I could trust him in very stoned situations. He and I would drive the equipment down to Morocco while John Porter and his woman Shadow would fly out with Chang and Digger, our sound engineers from Island. Reebop was a problem, though. He was on one of his famous binges at the time. I decided to steal his drums. I loaded them into *Shadowfax* with the rest of the recording equipment, called Reebop and told him that his drums were en route to Morocco, softening the blow by adding that there was a lump of cash in an envelope for him in the Island safe and that Suzette had his ticket.

'What's happening, man?'

I told him it was a surprise and that he'd better arrive in good shape as he was about to get involved with some serious African music. Dieter and I set off, with *Shadowfax* loaded down with expensive amps, speakers, a mixing-desk, Revoxes, microphones, stands, and Reebop's drums.

Dieter and I drove off the ferry into Tangiers. I tried to disguise the major items like the mixing-desk and the tape-recorders but Reebop's drums could not be hidden. We were a perfect target. A uniformed Customs man waved us down and indicated that we should get out. So I climbed from the cab and went reluctantly to the rear door as instructed. I was just about to open up for inspection when a Moroccan friend named Absalom appeared and spoke to the Customs officer briefly and waved me back into the cab. Then he climbed in and directed us out of the docks and onto the streets of Tangiers to the new house in Marchand, a rambling villa set in a mature garden with ponds and palm trees and a wonderful view over the Strait of Gibraltar.

The main salon, our studio, was a huge room with a

fireplace at each end and a frieze of Alhambra tiles. The salon had banquettes running around the walls, and several small, intricately decorated tables surrounded by low stools. Reebop's drums had been set up on the Berber rugs strewn in the centre. Chang, Digger, John Porter and Shadow were due to arrive the next day to set up the recording equipment. I had hand-picked the crew, all of whom could be relied upon to respect the G'naoua, their customs and culture. I slept confidently that first night.

The next day the G'naoua arrived *en masse* and, in the polite way that Moroccans have, checked things out. After a while the vibes gelled as the crew, the G'naoua, and all of their friends hung out. Music was the central topic. John Porter and Dieter shared a love of the blues. As a result, the house was rarely silent. Some of the younger G'naoua would jam with us, teaching us their rhythms on the bindir and saffi drums. Eventually, I felt comfortable and familiar enough to send for Reebop. I called Suzette at Island and asked her to give him his ticket and some spending money. I waited in suspense at Tangiers Airport. Finally he staggered through the arrivals gate, stink-faced drunk.

Reebop was a stocky five foot, and had powerful arms and hands as hard as stone, the result of millions of drum beats. It was touch and go at Immigration. Morocco is a Muslim country and alcohol is prohibited. I grabbed Reebop and pleaded his case: 'He's afraid of flying,' I explained, and somehow we got out of the airport and into *Shadowfax* and I drove around town and down to the beach at Cap Spartel to sober him up.

'Hey, brother, where's the action? Wine, man, where is the wine, man?'

'Reebop, this is a dope country. There's no booze allowed.'

He eventually fell asleep by a fire on the beach, courtesy of a couple of camping hippies. I knew the music would be in full swing back at the house, waiting to be joined by an

African king's drummer. And here he was, sleeping like a baby. I covered him up with a blanket and sat with him smoking kif with the bemused hippies. They had no idea who their sleeping guest was as they tapped away on their drums.

Then Reebop stirred.

'Hey, brother, what's happening? What the fuck is this?'

'Welcome to Morocco,' I said, giving Reebop a chillum of Achmed's finest hashish. Soon he was playing the drum and attracting attention as the camp-fire became surrounded by a crowd of drumming and fluting hippies. I finally dragged my drummer away and we arrived at the house.

The scent of jasmine and *dama de noche* wafted from the gardens and courtyard. Reebop returned to the real world. 'Nice place, my brother.' I took him through the house into the main salon where there were forty people in the large room. Candles and lanterns threw shadows on the ceiling and wall tiles. The dancing flames of the fire picked out the Berber faces peering from the small groups that sat around the room, drinking tea and smoking kif.

Reebop was bewildered at first. Then he saw his four congas in their stand, tuned and ready to go. The flames danced in anticipation, casting dim shadows onto the ceiling. Reebop approached his drums as if in a trance and started to tap, tap, tap: little riffs began popping from his fingers, then from his palms. As the sound increased the focus in the room turned towards the diminutive black drummer.

Reebop Kwaku Baah was one of the best percussionists in the world, up there with Mongo Santamaria and the best that Haiti and Africa could produce. With the rock and roll education he had received in London during the Sixties, he was a musical force. The room fell silent except for the slow rhythms that Reebop was playing. He was limbering up, showing off a bit. He loved an audience and was only truly happy when playing to a crowd. He lifted

202

his playing a gear or two, sensing the curiosity of the audience.

The master flute-player Mohammed Zain of the Jllala sect was at one of the tables with an old mountain Berber in a patched *djellaba*. The old man opened a cloth bag and took out an eighteen-inch-square drum, the like of which I had not seen before. It was like a picture frame with a tightly stretched skin on either side, inside which were a couple of drone strings. The old man took his drum over to the fire and squatted there, gently heating the instrument. Reebop continued playing, messing about, cracking rim shots and set-piece riffs into the room. He was not holding down any particular rhythm but he was making impressive sounds.

I sat at a table and watched Reebop's shadow dancing on the walls and ceiling. As I smoked some *sebsis* with Abdelkader, a second shadow appeared dancing with Reebop's. It was the old Berber with the strange square drum. The old man started to lay down a serious Berber rhythm. He played it unflinchingly and hypnotically into Reebop's face. As the sound bounced around the salon, I caught sight of Chang in the ante-chamber with earphones clamped over his head, looking lost in deep concentration. He pulled off the cans and beckoned me over: 'Listen to this.'

I put the cans on and listened. At first the ambience of the room breathed and crackled into my head: the fire, the whispering of the people, Reebop's drums, and the drum of the old man. All these sounds were perfectly audible; so was the babbling choir that sang over the general sound. I gave Chang the cans. 'That's spooky, man,' he said, putting the cans back on. We could hear a choir of voices where there wasn't one.

A hush descended, the pulsing red glow of the *sebsis* pipes illuminated dark corners of the room. Large beads of sweat started to form on Reebop's face and neck as the old man's rhythm cut into and across the riffs Reebop was playing. For some reason he was finding it difficult to settle. He continued to explore his drums – kwack, kwack, gadung, kwack. The sweat dripped from his chin. The hairs on the back of my neck prickled as I realized that this was an initiation not only for Reebop but for all the infidels in the room. The old man's drum continued relentlessly in a magnificent, metronomic, subtle, hypnotic, tonal Berber rhythm, the true magic of the drum unleashed. I looked around: Porter and Shadow sat stoned and mesmerized; Dicko was toking on a huge Jamaican-style spliff; Chang and Digger concentrated on the recording. Then Reebop stopped struggling with his drums and began to play the old man's riff right back to him.

Dieter had been particularly affected by the intensity of the ritual and the music. He had been putting the finishing touches on an instrument he had been constructing. It was his top-secret project, which he kept in a guitar case with 'Lucille' written on it out of reverence for his hero B.B. King. One morning Dieter solemnly announced that he had finished his *Kraftwerk* and invited us all to its unveiling. He wanted to do this in the Petit Socco. Dicko, Porter and Shadow, Abdellah and I drove down to the Café Centrale and took a table outside on the street. The maze of the medina branched away from us in all directions. We ordered tea and smoked our kif, listening to the hubbub and cacophony of an Arab market-place, the prevailing sound provided by the hundreds of radios in the boutiques, humming away.

Dieter opened his 'Lucille' box to reveal an instrument based on the shape of my wand, the caduceus: a rod, topped by a circle, topped by a half moon. Dieter had machine-tooled this instrument out of a solid chunk of aluminium he had cut from a crashed Starfighter in Germany many years before while doing military service. The tuning keys were set inside the crescent

204

moon, the strings ran down to the end of the rod. It made no acoustic sound as Dieter sat there playing in the café. Then he got up from the table saying, 'I'll be back,' and took off into the radio boutique. Minutes later he returned, still playing his silent blues. We noticed that the sound emanating from the radio shop was no longer Arabian music. It had been replaced by a funky blues.

Dieter had constructed one of the first transmitting guitars. It had a hundred-yard range and a frequency that could be picked up on any radio: all you had to do was twiddle the tuner until you found his sound. As Dieter played, we spread out tuning every radio in the vicinity to his concert. We were well known at the Café Centrale. Soon the locals realized what was happening and crowded around. Dieter was a genius, and thoroughly deserved the standing ovation that he and his impromptu concert got from the crowd in the medina.

Putzy spent a few days with us. She seemed all right but I detected a certain sadness. Of course, I tried to persuade her to stay – I was so pleased to see her and let her hear the G'naoua. Indeed, many friends came to visit and listen. And then it was time to leave. We had been privileged to witness a unique musical culture and to have had six weeks of Moroccan hospitality. Reebop had played his heart out in some memorable sessions and the G'naoua had given us a glimpse of their magical heritage. After one last night of feasting and music, the party was over. The Porters, Chang, Digger and Reebop flew back to London, while Dieter and I packed the equipment and loaded up *Shadowfax* with our precious recordings. The G'naoua gave us their blessing and waved us goodbye as we went aboard the ferry. The music was on its way.

We drove *Shadowfax* across Spain, satisfied at a job well done. Soon we would be back in London, where we hoped to mix an album from the recordings in the studio at St Peter's Square.

Dieter had never been to Granada so I made a detour and drove him up to the Alhambra and then to Sacramonte to visit a flamenco family who lived in the caves. I had lost the habit of drinking in Tangiers so the few glasses of wine we drank with the Gitanos must have affected my reactions. Anxious to get to Bilbao to catch our boat, we drove away from Granada, the echo of their music ringing in our ears.

The Sierra Nevada is an unforgiving mountain range with precarious roads that wind down to the plains of central Spain, twisting and turning over peaks and through gorges. It was a dark night and Spanish rain slopped down, turning the road into a mountain river. I had driven thousands of miles in *Shadowfax* and had never had so much as a close shave.

The small landslide caught me by surprise. I saw the rocks as I turned a bend, quickly changed down and braked, a dark chasm to my right and a torrent of water spilling across the road to my left. Quite gently the back end of *Shadowfax* started to skid away from me. I adjusted the steering and drove into the skid. It was all quite calm. Dieter said, 'Here we go,' as the back end swished around, the wheels dropped off the mountain road. There was no wall or railing to stop it. I gripped the wheel and through the windscreen watched the full beams of my headlights climb slowly up the side of the mountain and into the sky until all I could see was two tubes of light disappearing into black infinity. JJ Cale was singing to us as we started to fall backwards. Some of the gorges dropped hundreds of feet into ravines, others were quite gentle slopes. I had no idea which kind we were falling into. The first crash was loud and quite shocking; the truck tipped up, and then fell free, crashed and bounced, and fell again, all in slow-motion. JJ's rhythm guitar chugged on. Crash, thud – then total darkness and silence except for the slap of the rain and the final revolutions of the Land-Rover's wheels.

Amazingly I was alive. I knew this because my finger hurt.

I lay on my side in the total darkness, my face pressed against the driver's door. I reached out and called, 'Dieter, are you okay?' I waited for a sound.

'Yeah, man. I'm okay. Far out, man, that was far out.'

Rain was belting down, and yet we were both completely dry in our mountain *djellabas*. It seemed sensible to stay where we were since there was nothing we could do in the dark and wet. The diesel fumes worried us though, so we refrained from lighting a joint. Instead, Dieter produced a couple of mandrax from his drug tin and we both crashed out.

When I came to, I saw a beautiful valley through the upturned windscreen. The truck was on its side. The carawagon roof had been ripped off, spilling the contents of *Shadowfax* out on the mountainside as we had fallen and rolled. We climbed out to survey the damage. Dieter found his 'Lucille' case, which had been speared by a mike-stand. The heavy metal rod had gone clean through its side. He looked as if he was holding an injured child. He slowly pulled out the offending spear, and opened the case. 'Lucille' was unscathed, as was my precious Martin in its fibreglass case; my flute collection was also intact. I walked up the mountain looking through the wreckage. Reebop's drum cases were strewn about with other flight cases, but they were unharmed. My beautifully carved white marble Jain Buddha had crashed out of the truck and was sitting peacefully the right way up on the mountainside, as if watching over us.

But the most miraculous discovery of all was the box of recordings. There were two dozen twelve-inch tapes in a cardboard box which had been protected from the rain by the ripped-off roof.

We were eventually spotted and the Guardia Civil arrived on the scene. They wanted us to leave the truck and everything in it where it was, and go with them back to Granada. I was streaming tears because, as I discovered later, I had been sprayed with battery acid during the crash and my clothes were slowly rotting.

Organizing the retrieval of our belongings, recording equipment, Reebop's drums and all the rest of *Shadowfax*'s equipment was a nightmare. But finally the truck and all its contents were towed out of the ravine and placed in a secure garage in Granada. Could this be the end of my beloved *Shadowfax*? Dieter and I hired a van and finished our journey.

We arrived at St Peter's Square exhausted and battered, but triumphant. I spent the next few months editing and mixing the album, which we called *Trance, Kwaku Baah G'naoua*. It was eventually put out on Island Records and was one of World Music's first commercial releases.

The release of the record was an anticlimax for me. I felt that my journey was over; *Shadowfax* was as good as dead in Granada. And Putzy was deep in a new life. Michael Pearson had left England to be a temporary tax exile in Ibiza.

I was suffering from the common condition of returned travellers, an identity crisis. I was looking for a way to re-enter the material world. I had learned a lot on my travels, but I had come back with a magnificent naïveté. Most of the contemporaries I had left behind had continued to work nine to five, and most had achieved the rewards that come from such endeavours. Some had even found job satisfaction. A new decade was looming. Old hippies were two a penny on the Portobello Road.

Shortly after returning from Morocco with the tapes, I gave Dieter a few hundred pounds. He had wanted to go back to Granada. I gave him the papers to *Shadowfax* and told him that if he could salvage anything from the wreck he could have it. Dieter went off to live with the Gitanos in Sacramonte with his crazy guitar to study flamenco.

One day I was lying in bed in a room above the travel agent in the Portobello Road, aptly named Gandalf's Travels, when I was awoken by a continuous horn blasting, in a rhythm I recognized as G'naoua. I thought that I was dreaming. I climbed out of bed and went to the window. There in the street was *Shadowfax* and the smiling face of Dieter.

I ran down to the street as he stood with the keys dangling from his fingers. I gave him a hug, and immediately jumped behind the wheel. How he had driven back from Spain I do not know. The chassis was bent, which gave the truck a crab-like gait. The steering-box was loose, the roof had been put back on but was so damaged that several gaps and tears let in daylight. But the old truck was back on the road. We drove through the market, just like old times. Dieter hung around for a while but was not yet ready for city life. To this day I do not know where he went, or what became of him.

Chapter Thirty

Dieter's wonderful gift cheered me a little. Philip Harvey had a funky VW bus, so I joined him with the gallant *Shadowfax* and we formed a small convoy and took off into the heart of England.

We travelled around England and Wales discovering many settlements of fellow travellers; the New Age movement was suddenly alive. Sid Rawles, self-appointed Druid chieftain, camped out with his tribe on the Wiltshire Downs. Tipi settlements sprang up, some in Wiltshire, some in Wales. All the country fairs became mini-festivals. The summer of 1977 was great, with no bureaucracy or police controls. We were absolutely free to travel. For the most part, New Age travellers at this time were conscientious hippies with a love of the countryside, the environment and the culture. Farmers welcomed us onto their land, and the small communities that we passed through treated us with polite curiosity. We could camp in the circles of Stonehenge or Avebury. We cleaned up when we left a place. Travelling the ley lines was an adventure. I was now exploring England and my own culture and found that its traditions and folklore were very much alive. Some of the smaller fairs in Suffolk and Norfolk provided gathering places for the exchange of ideas, crafts, music and, of course, dope.

I drifted back into a gypsy existence, often alone, sometimes with a group of travellers. I would make the odd visit to London, but I was not ready to rejoin society. I had no money, no job. I was living out of a beat-up Land-Rover.

I reached my lowest ebb when on one of my visits to London an old friend, Sabrina Guinness, invited me to a party. It was full of people I hadn't seen for years. A rather select card game had sprung up in a back room and I sat in. Eric Clapton and Ronnie Wood were there. It was a small game for fun and fivers, and I don't know why to this day, but I dealt myself a card from the bottom of the deck to win a hand, perhaps for the adrenalin rush of doing something naughty, or perhaps because I was desperate and broke. I don't know. But to my shame I pocketed the winnings. It was the first and only time I cheated at cards. I prided myself on being an honest gambler. The event depressed me and played on my mind.

A few days later I had to call John Porter about something. He was staying at Eric Clapton's house. Eric answered the phone.

'Hi,' I said. 'It's Mim.'

There was a pause, then Eric said quite matter of factly: 'Still cheating at cards, Mim?'

I was gutted. I couldn't get any lower. I had to pull myself together. This was not the life I'd been searching for. I remembered the words of Sufi sage Faisal Ayaz: 'Do not seek these three things, for you will seek them in vain: a man of knowledge whose deeds correspond with his knowledge, a man of action whose heart accords with his deeds, and a fellow human-being with no failings.'

Then I received a message from Michael Pearson. He was about to marry 'Fritzy' Ellen Erhardt, and wanted to take her on a pre-wedding trip to Morocco. Could I pick up his Range-Rover and meet them in Tangiers? Glad of a sponsored drive, I agreed. Soon I was back in familiar territory. I collected Michael and Fritzy in Tangiers, after first visiting the Café of the Cats to see Abdullah Sphinx (I had retired him there on my last trip). He had sired many kittens and was now the leader of the Hiafa cat-pack. The three of us had a great trip, visiting all my favourite places, driving as far south as Tarfia and exploring the Moyen Atlas. I eventually put Michael and Fritzy on a plane in Marrakech. Michael suggested that I take my time bringing the car home.

I spent a while in Marbella with Gavin, then drove through France to St-Tropez. I had a bad feeling about Putzy. I had not heard from her and she was not returning my calls. We had never had a problem communicating before, even though she was now in a new relationship. It was possible that Michael had forbidden her to talk to me, but it was not in her nature to be dictated to. I drove with mixed feelings along the bamboo roadway that skirted the bay of Canubier, past Brigitte Bardot's house, over the gravel and into Putzy's drive.

There were no cars in the car park. I pushed open the thick oak door in the perimeter wall and looked once more down at the beautiful garden that her mother had lovingly laid out in the Fifties. The house was unchanged, the pink stone gleamed in the sunlight. Through the arches I could see the boats bobbing in the private harbour. As I approached the main house Vanya, Putzy's cocker spaniel, came up to me sniffing her way along the path, her long ears almost trailing along the ground. There was no barking, just sniffing. She gave my hand a lick and then led the way through the house, and out again onto the sun-deck. There was Putzy lying on a sun-bed with a pile of books. She was alone in the house so we were able to spend a few days together catching up on our lives. I would have loved to have taken her with me, but it was not to be. So I headed back to London to start a new life. I had to find some work or go mad.

There was a young musician called Andy Colquhoun who hung around the Portobello Road. He had put together a band called the Warsaw Pakt with John Walker, Lucas Fox, Chris

Underhill, and vocalist Jimmy Coul. I happened to walk past their rehearsal basement one evening. The raw sound of New Wave punk pounded up through a trapdoor in the pavement. I sat and listened for a while. Eventually, I went down and introduced myself.

For some time I'd harboured the vision of making instant records. I felt strongly that if a band or musician could play live then he or she should be able to record live. And the best and cheapest way to record live was to cut the sound directly onto vinyl. Digital recording and CDs were still some years in the future. In those days, recordings were mastered from tape to a cutting lathe. The lathe transformed the information on the tape into a vibration that ran through the machine into a minute diamond cutting head. This head was then lowered in the same way as the needle on a record player, except that instead of playing the groove, the sharp vibrating needle cut into a virgin acetate disc. This disc would then become the master from which all copies of the record would be made. The process was comparatively uncomplicated.

Normally, the sound that goes to the lathe is already recorded on tape to the satisfaction of everyone involved. I wanted to dispense with tape recording altogether and record a band directly to the cutting lathe. This presented several problems. The cutting head on the lathe is very sensitive and any minute abnormality in the sound would cause the diamond to make an exaggerated jump into a neighbouring groove, just like a scratched record does. The other problem was how to make a whole album directly to disc. It required the band to play the entire side of the album perfectly, all the way through without stopping, in one continuous groove. With the Warsaw Pakt this would mean recording seven tracks nonstop, in tune, and perfectly performed.

I spent some time working out whether this could be done or not. The advantages – if I could pull it off – were fantastic. The climate of the music on the streets at this time was immediate. Punk was at its zenith. If a band could take what it played tonight and put it on the market tomorrow morning in the form of an instantly recorded record, they would be hot.

The standard process of making a record took many months by comparison. Also, the cost of a direct-to-disc recording would be a fraction of the cost of a studio album. Many young bands could benefit from this method of recording. It was an alternative way for them to get a record into the marketplace until they could make a proper record deal. I put my idea to the Pakt. They liked it. It would be a first. They had the confidence and the musicianship to pull it off. I started work on pulling together a crew.

I went to my friend John Porter and asked him to oversee the sound. Next I needed a really good man on the live mix in the studio. For this I recruited the amiable Hutch. He was the chief back-line engineer for all Island Records' live gigs. I needed a cheap studio with a cutting lathe on the premises. This I found at Soho's Trident Studios.

I would set up a stage in the ground-floor studio and mike up the band as if for a live gig. Hutch would be responsible for mixing this sound in the room, and then he would be expected to send a stereo mix of the ambient sound plus all the other feeds to the desk in Studio Two, where John Porter would receive everything. Porter would make a live stereo mix and send his two-track creation up to me. I was to wait for it at the cutting lathe. I would be watching the diamond cutting its thin curl of vinyl from the smooth shining black disc. (You have to drive the lathe while looking down a microscope. It is essential that the operator does not allow one groove to touch the next. One touch and we would have to start recording the whole side of the album again.)

When this was set up I went to Chris Blackwell for the money. The projected costs were nothing in comparison to a regular album. Chris said, 'If you think you can do it, do it.'

The most important thing was to ensure that the Pakt were well rehearsed, so we locked them away to hone the songs and to get used to playing seven of them in tune, without a break. This required spare instruments for each track. Unlike a concert which unfolds at its own pace, with pauses and breaks and ad-libs, the making of a direct-to-disc album needed strict discipline. There is only so much room on the side of a vinyl record, and if we ran over even by seconds we would have to re-record.

Soon I had a date, a time and a place. I made a schedule of events and published this as a two-page ad in the *Melody Maker* and the *New Musical Express*. It described the schedule of Operation Needle Time. If all went well we would start the recording at midnight, and I planned to put five thousand Warsaw Pakt albums in the shops first thing in the morning. The band and their friends were to make the album sleeves. I had several rubber stamps and stencils made; these would be used on blank sleeves. This would add to the uniqueness of the finished record: no two album sleeves would be the same.

D-Day arrived. We threw a party in the studio prior to the recording session. The Trident Studios building was crammed with friends, liggers and press. Right on schedule, at the stroke of midnight, the Warsaw Pakt smashed into their first song. The atmosphere was fantastic, Hutch mixed an incredible sound in the main studio. He fired his mixes up to Porter, who did his bit cleaning up the live tracks as he received them. He also had to equalize the sound and reduce it to a stereo mix, which he fired up to me. I received this at the cutting lathe, sitting on a swivel stool, not unlike an anti-aircraft emplacement. With one eye glued to the microscope, I watched and listened to the record taking shape. We had one false start when the cutting needle jumped off the disc as a string broke on Andy's guitar. Apart from that mishap we recorded both sides without a pause.

As soon as the recording was finished I ran with the acetates to a waiting car and sped to Haringay where a pressing plant was waiting to receive the masters. While I did this the band and friends sat in the Kilburn flat of the Grey brothers, stamping and stencilling the album sleeves. I arrived with the pressed records at six o'clock in the morning. We slipped the first thousand into their sleeves and rushed them around London to a selection of pre-arranged independent record shops. I also had runners deliver the record with press releases to all the radio stations: 'The Fastest Album in the World'. We hadn't bothered with the *Guinness Book of Records*, but we knew what we had achieved. By nine in the morning, the Warsaw Pakt were getting airplay and selling copies of a record that hadn't existed the night before. We soon sold out of our original pressing, and *Needle Time* by the Warsaw Pakt became a post-punk collector's item.

The other feature of the record was its sound quality. Because we hadn't used tape, there was no degeneration of sound from the instruments to the diamond on the cutting lathe. The record sounded remarkably live. The Warsaw Pakt went on to become a cult band in London until the untimely death of the rhythm guitarist, John Walker.

Chapter Thirty-one

As a result of *Needle Time*, I acquired an unofficial desk in the war room at Island Records in 1977, which evolved into the position of head of marketing. I formed a company within Island which we called Yo-Yo, its main function to exploit and merchandise the considerable archive of artwork that the company had acquired over the years – incredible album sleeves, photographs and graphics, some of which were rock and roll icons. I worked closely with the art department.

Island was going through a quiet phase and needed a big hit. It would come from an unusual source. Famous for its innovation in nurturing reggae, the studio signed a band called the Buggles. Their first record, 'Video Killed the Radio Star', was an instant hit and went straight to number one. This success meant a new lease of life for Island, and a great run of hits followed. Bob Marley was rehearsing with his band in the rehearsal room at the back of the St Peter's Square building. Marianne Faithfull, the B-52s, Robert Palmer, Ultravox, Eddie and the Hot Rods, Grace Jones and JJ Cale were suddenly all getting hit records. The atmosphere in the war room was fantastic.

Mark Miller-Mundy had just produced an album with Marianne Faithfull for Island, the best album she had ever made. It was a brilliant record and deserved to go all the way, but sadly this was not going to happen in England. The BBC and EMI banned it because of the 'suck your cock' line in the lyrics. Chris Blackwell asked me if I would take Marianne and her band over to New York to oversee her appearance on *Saturday Night Live*, a show that went out live to thirty million people and could make or break an artist. Island needed an American hit. Marianne's *Broken English* might just be it. She had not been in the charts for many years.

Marianne put a band together with the very talented Barry Reynolds, and the chemistry worked. As head of marketing I had been working with photographer Dennis Morris on the artwork; he had come up with a terrific album sleeve and graphics. Several tracks were destined to be cult hits, most notably the title-track 'Broken English' and 'The Ballad of Lucy Jordan'.

At this time Marianne was, by her own admission, a naughty girl. Her capacity to abuse was well known. My first job was to see that rehearsals happened, and that Marianne was healthy. This meant no drink or drugs.

Marianne was always a wonderful mix of lady and tramp. Her choice of clothes, if choice is the word, was classic. No woman in the world could wear a pair of broken-heeled shoes as sexily. In scuffed leather trousers and matching blouson, she was a junkie's dream-girl. This, together with the siren call of her incredible speaking and singing voice, made her the female icon of British rock and roll.

But I was trying to spoil her fun. My first job was to freeze out any bad company – not easy. She was a sensible lady and soon came round to understanding the importance of the impending gig. The rehearsals started to take shape. Marianne cut down on everything and soon appeared to be in good form. The day came for us to hit the road. In typical British style we all piled into minicabs to the airport. The New York end was a different story. We were met by the NBC limo service. The driver, used to driving John Belushi and Co., was immediately offering us supplies. This was not going to be an easy assignment. I told the limo driver that his extra services were not required.

218

We checked into our hotel. In the lobby the Faithfull band waited for the elevator. When it arrived, the doors opened to reveal Anita Pallenberg. The two rock *femmes* fell into each other's arms screaming and shrieking with delight. Anita looked a little different from the Barbarella beauty I remembered from Villefranche, having gained a couple of stone since leaving Keith; these two remarkable women made an exotic sight. Up we went to Anita's apartment for what I hoped would be a courtesy call, but soon the gathering had turned into a party, which I had to struggle to escape from. I finally got Marianne away before too much damage was done.

We were followed from Anita's apartment by a little man who owned the Mud Club. He wanted Marianne to do a gig for him. Anita was all for it. I checked out the Mud Club and found it to be on its last legs, in need of a boost. Marianne had never played a live gig in NY, so her debut would be a valuable prize. With persuasion from her New York friends, Marianne decided to do it.

I organized rehearsals at NBC for Marianne and the band, and while this was happening made a deal with the Mud Club, which had a capacity of four hundred. There were no big bucks to be made, just a little bit of rock and roll history.

I made the club pay more than it could afford because the run-off in street cred would more than compensate for the loss made on the night. Part of the deal was that the press would be restricted, and that there be only word-of-mouth promotion. It was going to be no problem selling four hundred tickets to New York's *cognoscenti*. It was arranged that Marianne should play at midnight, directly after the *Saturday Night Live* show.

Back at NBC, rehearsals were going well. Marianne and the band were happening and we were all in high spirits. I reported this back to Island Records and Warner Brothers, Marianne's US distributor. *Saturday Night Live* had a massive following; in fact it was the biggest live TV show in the US. Its gang of stars,

219

with whom the guests interacted, included John Belushi, Dan Ackroyd and Chevy Chase, who were at this time an awesome, hip comedy team.

Into the huge studio we went for rehearsal, Marianne in biker jacket and scuffed-heeled boots, slouching in behind her band to do her thing. Click! On came the red light. She was singing and sounding great. At the end of her rehearsal the studio broke into applause, technicians, stage hands, lighting guys up in the gantry, all welcoming a truly Marianne performance. We went to bed that night in euphoric relief. Marianne shared out the cash advance from the Mud Club. It was hard to believe that an artist of her calibre in the late Seventies could have no money. Hopefully this *SNL* show was going to be the catalyst to change all that.

I awoke early. It was showday. I had breakfast with the band and the car came and took us to the studio. We'd planned to spend the day in the NBC building. We rehearsed a bit, had lunch, and did a full run-through. Marianne sang her two songs brilliantly. For the run-through we'd taken delivery of three foxy backing-singers, courtesy of Mark Miller-Mundy; as producer of Marianne's record, he felt they would enhance the performance.

I left Marianne alone in her large star's dressing-room for a few minutes while I talked to the director. I returned to her dressing-room to find it empty. I went next door to the girls. There they were doing their fine faces in the burning light of their mirrors.

'Have you seen Marianne?'

'Sure, honey, she's in the john.'

Oh, no! I tapped on the door. 'Marianne?' No reply. I tapped again. 'Marianne?'

A very slurred croaky voice responded, 'Whaddya wan?'

I opened the door. Marianne was sitting on the loo fully dressed, with a bottle of brandy between her knees. She was out of it, with only three hours to showtime. I got Marianne back to her dressing-room where she cursed me, not maliciously but like a naughty child. I got her to lie down and hoped that she had time to sleep off whatever she had taken. I was going to look for a friendly doctor. There was an aggressive knock on the door. Oh, shit. I opened the door to Mick Jagger. He appeared to be a little drunk and was probably having a nice New York day. Maybe he was in the NBC building on business and someone told him that Marianne was in dressing-room twelve. He had not seen her since she was carried away from him on a stretcher after their break-up during the *Ned Kelly* film. I knew that she would love to see him, particularly with her record high in the charts.

'Hello, Scala, can I see Marianne?'

'Sorry, Mick, not right now. She would love to see you, can I arrange it for later?'

Mick was not pleased. We were standing in the doorway having an argument about his entry. It was crazy. I couldn't tell him she was unconscious on a bed from too much brandy and procaine. I knew she would not want her first meeting with him in ages to be like this. So I stuck to my guns.

The situation was getting desperate when, as if by magic, Madame Jo Bergman appeared, a real pro, who at this time was in charge of special projects at Warner Brothers. She used to run the Rolling Stones office in London; she also knew me. She quickly sussed the situation and calmly guided Mick away.

Minutes later she returned. 'What was that all about, Mim?' I explained the need for a doctor. She made a couple of quick calls, and within minutes, John Belushi's doctor arrived. He was a man of experience. Marianne was soon feeling much better, ready to go to work. The director had heard something was up and came to see for himself. After a brief chat he went away, satisfied that she could perform. He offered to let her cut one of the songs from her set. 'No, no,' she insisted. 'I'm fine.' We were close to blowing *Saturday Night Live*.

Showtime. I followed Marianne, the band and the backing girls into the wings of the studio stage, now crammed with a full audience. Chevy Chase introduced Marianne as the female icon of British rock and roll. The band played and Marianne sang 'Broken English'. She got through it well enough but we all knew she was a bit shaky. On the other hand she always looked vulnerable when she performed.

Like a true pro she pulled it off. I watched with Mark Miller-Mundy, who was panicking, but the audience did not need cue cards to applaud: they loved her. Marianne staggered off the stage and collapsed into a chair in her dressing-room. The director came rushing in.

'You were fantastic. Can you handle the second song?'

'Of course I can,' croaked Marianne, her voice ominous. The show went on. A couple of funny sketches with Chase and Ackroyd, and it was time for song number two. Marianne sashayed onto the stage, and sang the guts out of the next song. It was over. Marianne had performed her new record to thirty million people; we could relax. Or could we? In the dressing-room after the show Marianne's voice finally gave out and was reduced to a hoarse whisper.

We had to go to the after-show reception, as I had arranged for Jo Bergman to bring Mick along. Marianne sat with Mick as cast and crew celebrated the end of one more Saturday night. Finally it was time to go to the Mud Club. Marianne assured me she wanted to go ahead with the gig, which was just as well, as she and the band had spent the advance. The band, Marianne and I climbed into one huge car and led the way. Other cars followed us downtown to Soho. As we approached the Mud Club, it became obvious that word of mouth and watchers of *SNL* had spread within the N.Y. junkie community.

It was impossible to get within a block of the club. The

manager had let in the first four hundred people at twelve and it was now one in the morning. We entered the Mud Club via an industrial elevator of a clothes factory a block away, and clambered along the New York skyline over rooftops, past pigeon-lofts. I had arranged for us to have the top floor of the Mud building. It was a big loft space and soon filled up with characters: Anita and her gang, some people from the show, friends of mine and Marianne, and scary New York freaks. Her voice was disappearing.

I went downstairs to check things out. The place was bedlam. Every possible space was jam-packed – the stairwell, the anterooms, the reception area and the club itself were all loaded to capacity. The manager was on the door refusing entry, and enjoying the Mud Club's revival. It was the place to be that night.

We took an industrial lift down to the stage. The steel shutters clanked open, revealing the club to us, a smoke-filled inferno, dark as a dungeon. Terry Stanard found his drum kit and immediately got a shuffle going. Joe Maverty walked on stage with his guitar. Soon the rest of the band fell in with him while Marianne had a few croaked words with her friend Anita. Anita wore a lot of fur and must have been steaming hot as she and her mates dropped down into the pit at the front of the stage. I stood in the wings with a girl who was a rock stringer for *Rolling Stone* magazine. We watched Marianne venture across the stage to outrageous applause of the punters. This was rock and roll, it didn't come any rockier.

Someone at the front of the stage offered Marianne a drink from a nondescript bottle; she took it and gave it a swig but puked it at the side of the stage. Then, pulling herself together, microphone in hand, the swallow tattoo that flies across the back of her left hand fluttering, she apologized to the frenzied crowd in a broken whisper: 'I'm afraid I have lost my voice.'

The crowd didn't care, they were in for the rock and roll

223

and were going to get it. Marianne swayed across the stage, gently put down the bottle and whispered 'Sister Morphine' to Stanard. The band opened up. Marianne then croaked out a scorching version of the song. She sang it, she was it, Sister Morphine was on stage.

The amplification wasn't great, but it didn't matter. The crowd was gone. The *Rolling Stone*'s reporter gripped my arm with excitement, blown away. Mark Miller-Mundy ran out of the club in horror, complaining that the sound was terrible. The concert ended and we all retired to party into the wee hours. Back at our hotel, mission accomplished, I began to relax. We put Marianne to bed; she was exhausted, and had done a great day's work.

Not everyone was happy. Miller-Mundy thought Marianne's career was in trouble, but a great *Rolling Stone* review of the gig dispelled his fears.

I slept on the plane back to London. The album *Broken English* reached number eighty-two in the US charts, enough to re-establish Marianne and to bring her to a new audience.

Chapter Thirty-two

Shadowfax was stolen from a parking meter in Battersea, never to be seen again. The Eighties were here. I went back to work, unscathed by my adventures, and certainly enriched.

Once I had decided to come off the road, as it were, re-entry was not that bad. My friends helped me. Simon Kirk, the drummer with Bad Company, and his beautifully crazy American-Italian wife, Desirée, came to the rescue. Bad Company and Led Zeppelin were now managed by the infamous Peter Grant (my fellow Macedonian warrior in *Cleopatra*). I had been out of touch with mainstream music, and Desirée and Simon took it upon themselves to reintroduce me. Pushed by Desirée, I began managing again.

I started working with James Lascelles and Michael Story, who had a jazzy but totally uncommercial band called Cuckoo, an offshoot of the Global Village Trucking Company, and the Breakfast Band. I loved their music, so I released their album *Iona* and moved into No. 1 Orme Lane with them. The house shared a garden with James's mother, the concert pianist Marion Stein, and his stepfather Jeremy Thorpe. By the end of the Eighties, Michael had become a highly successful composer of film and television scores.

Soon I had a new office courtesy of the music business accountant David Simmons. He gave me space alongside his Leosong Company in Charlotte Street. Together we formed ESP Music and Management Ltd. We had a simple deal. I

225

would do my thing, he would do the paperwork, and we would split the proceeds down the middle. This was the best business partnership I had ever made. David's back-up allowed me once again to do what I loved best: encouraging talented people to be creative. ESP grew rapidly into the first agency solely to represent record producers. My first client, Chris Kimsey, had engineered several albums for the Rolling Stones, including *Emotional Rescue*. I felt he warranted a producer credit and negotiated one for him with Prince Rupert. He was also associate producer with the Glimmer Twins on *Tattoo You*.

Chris and I had some great musical adventures together in the Eighties, including a magical four months in Jamaica under the auspices of the legendary Danny Simms. Danny recorded Bob Marley when he was a young Jamaican musician trying to make a living as a singer with his band in New York in the Sixties. When Danny started to release this music in the Eighties, at a time when Bob had become the Rastafarian icon, purists in the industry felt that Danny should have kept the old Marley material to himself. Naturally, Island Records did not want the material released, nor did Warner Brothers. They took out full-page ads in the music press disclaiming any connection with the Marley/Simms recordings.

Danny lived in New York at this time, managing those two other reggae masters, Jimmy Cliff and Peter Tosh. Chris was just finishing *Tattoo You* for the Stones. When I pestered Danny to let him produce the next Cliff album, Danny fixed me up with an introduction. In January 1982 I flew to Kingston with several boxes of spare parts for Peter Tosh's BMW and a plan to persuade Cliff and Tosh to let Chris produce their next albums. My old friend Dicko met me at the airport, and soon I was on a helter-skelter, Rasta, ganja drive into Trenchtown.

The Channel One studio looked from the outside more like a bunker than a cathedral of reggae music. It was surrounded by high railings and wire grilles. I stood in the back streets

226

of Trenchtown with my Rasta escort waiting for the grille to be unlocked. A crude mural of Bob Marley decorated the whole front of the building. Urchins played with a baby pig on a lead in the gutter outside. Soon someone with a bunch of keys appeared and let us in.

I walked from the blinding sunlight into a different world – the smoke-filled gloom of a primitive control room. Scientist was at the mixing desk. Through the window Cliff and his band were in full cry. I spent the next twelve hours listening to songs and gently persuading Cliff to let Kimsey produce them. That night I was able to call London and tell Chris to catch the next plane to Kingston. Once again I found myself in the midst of incredible music, as I sat with Kimsey in the ganja smoke of Channel One watching him produce the *Special* album for Jimmy Cliff and cutting the classic 'Johnny Be Good' track for Peter Tosh.

Some time later I heard a few tracks by a little girl from Rochdale. She was fourteen and came to London to see me. The songs were not great but the voice was. It was obvious that the child was a prodigy. Her name was Lisa Stansfield. I took her and her young producers to Polydor and made a deal with them to release Lisa's first single, with an option for her first album; after releasing it, incredibly, the A&R man in charge of the project couldn't see her potential, and dropped her. Four years later she recorded her debut album *Big Thing* for her Rocking Horse label. Its phenomenal success gave me immense pleasure.

In 1982 I started to manage that itinerant minstrel Eric Burdon ('I used to be an Animal but I'm all right now'). He had long left the Animals, and had formed War, with some success. He now sang in small clubs from Hamburg to Pasadena, the rough blues voice still there – a black boy in a white skin – never happier than when he was on stage with a blues band behind him.

For a bit of nostalgia, we reformed the Animals. The original break-up of the band in 1966 had left the relationships between this bunch of Geordies in tatters, and Alan Price with the credit and publishing royalties from 'The House of the Rising Sun'. Chas Chandler had gone on to manage Jimi Hendrix for a short time and eventually became a successful record-producer with Slade. The rest of the band – Eric, Hilton Valentine, and Johnny Steel – didn't profit from the original line-up, so to get the fivesome to even talk to each other required major acts of diplomacy.

After much cantankerous negotiation, with Rod Wynberg, John Price and myself as referees, the Animals were temporarily reformed. The subsequent album *Ark*, released on Miles Copeland's IRS label, was moderately successful in the US. The tour of America and Canada that followed, and the Geordie madness it entailed, could have inspired *Spinal Tap*, as we cruised the backbars and backwoods of New England and farther afield, while Vietnam vets proffered bags of grass in homage to their hero.

My next client was my old friend Stewart Levine. Boy George, Wham, Paul Young and Sade were selling millions of records. The sound they were trying to achieve was something that Stewart did naturally, honed from years of producing the Crusaders, B.B. King, Minnie Ripperton and Hugh Masekela. I suggested he work in England with the young R&B bands. He agreed and came to London in 1984 to give it a try. As a result, Stewart made some fabulous records with ESP, including the debut albums of Simply Red for Elektra and of the brilliant, ill-fated Curiosity Killed the Cat, whose front man Ben Volpelière was the son of my old Fifties jiving partner Belinda and *HMS Defiant* mucker, Jean Claude.

By now the record business was getting dodgy. The age of Stock, Aitken and Waterman was dawning. Machines were

228

replacing the minstrels. This was no place for me. It was time to go fishing.

In 1987 I sold out and moved to a quiet little county in Ireland where, with my new and only wife, we enjoy the exploits of our Irish-born son Freddie, a menagerie of animals, and the peace and quiet of a rural idyll where I can write and paint, and try to cast a fly the way Charles Ritz taught me on that small high lake in the Engadin. And, of course, I cock an ear to the radio whenever I hear a piece of real music muscle its way through the playlist system.

I have survived the drugs and the travels. The planet has become a much smaller place since I made my journeys. The use of the Internet and the Discovery Channel, and the vast collections of World Music in high-street shops, now regularly bring other cultures and customs into our homes. Over the next millennium we may come to tolerate and understand the diversity of thinking between peoples and religions, enabling us to live together in harmony, and with respect for our inquisitive natures and individualities.